Climbing the Mountain

The Heart of Budgeting

Wade J. Carey

Climbing the Mountain

The Heart of Budgeting

Wade J. Carey

Climbing The Mountain

the heart of budgeting

Copyright © 2018

by Wade J. Carey

Library of Congress Control Number:

ISBN: 1975656032

ISBN: 978-1975656034

For more information on author Wade J. Carey, visit www.wadejcarey.com

Printed in the United States of America by Kindle Direct Publishing

Cover design by: Rachel Bostwick   Interior artwork by: Rachel Bostwick

Interior layout by: Rachel Bostwick

Edited by: Cheryl Tengelsen

Certain stock imagery for the following chapter headings are used by permission from www.bigstockphoto.com: Prayer of Salvation, Biblical Verses Used

Table of Contents

Introduction

Hello, friends. Thanks for stopping by! I'm so glad you've joined me today. Since the subject of budgeting is such a difficult and sometimes controversial topic to discuss, let me start off by explaining what you can expect to discover between these pages.

At its core, this book is my personal testimony. It is neither intended to prescribe nor cure any specific financial ills. It is also not designed to provide any detailed financial growth techniques. Many others have excellent programs for those endeavors, and I have no desire at this time to reinvent the wheel. Essentially, what you're about to read is not a "how to" guide for your personal finances. But rather, it's an attempt to explain "why" you should create and/or manage an effective budget for the rest of your life.

The impetus behind the writing of this book is basically an examination of my own heart as I went through many experiences with the basics of budgeting over the years. As I look back on my various travails with money, I can see very clearly how my previously negative attitude towards budgeting had invasive, spiritually dangerous tendrils which penetrated far into my soul. In my estimation, that situation is true for many of you, also.

My goal in sharing this information is that I hope it will help you to find some spiritual peace and comfort in some way, shape, or form, as you deal with the frustrating subject of budgeting. Trust me when I tell you; budgeting is the keystone to maintaining balanced financial success and is the absolute nexus of your financial life. This book is merely an attempt to emphasize this opinion by the sharing of my various financial experiences in life so far. By the time you finish, you can obviously then decide for yourself if what I have to say has any merit.

Most of the concepts contained within these pages are things I've learned over the years through practical experience and much trial and error. Therefore, what I have to say is empirical, by nature. Although I'm not presenting these experiences and opinions within the context of a financial course—or as a magic bullet which will take you from financial pain to overflowing wealth—I do feel like you can glean something important by taking your valuable time to read and absorb what is being presented.

Honestly, in far too many cases, I've observed others painting the spiritual and heart-related aspects of how we approach the subject of budgeting with far too broad of a brush. This "one size fits all" approach to budgeting seems to me to be woefully inadequate for any long-term or sustained financial success. Actually, I feel that it's inadequate for _any_ type of financial success. I'll endeavor to convince you of this opinion as you're reading along.

After walking through and surviving many financial difficulties over the years, I've come to believe that our heart for budgeting is perhaps the most important function of our financial life. The techniques you'll learn in a personal finances course are incredibly valuable, but they're incomplete without the vital leadership from the conductor of one's own, personal financial orchestra—our "inner budgeter." Or as I like to call it, our internal "budgeting dude." For those of you who think you cannot connect to this inner persona in your soul, I believe you're mistaken. He or she is there, you just need to find them and allow them to do their job. Oftentimes, there are many distractions blocking a clear view of one's heart for budgeting. I'm going to try to help you clear the obstacles away.

As it relates to budgeting overall, I feel that gaining mere knowledge of the techniques on how to run a budget without the necessary wisdom on how to apply these techniques is largely useless. It's been said that only those who are humble in spirit pray for and seek wisdom. I agree with that. To my own way of thinking, mere financial knowledge without the necessary wisdom on how to apply it practically in your life is certainly useless in the case of your personal budget. It doesn't take a brainiac to become the master of your finances—it takes a common-sense budgeter.

As stated, there are many who have full-fledged financial courses which go into much further detail about how to build your personal finances on a solid platform with excellent techniques. Overall, these courses are a fantastic way to gain some wonderful knowledge. I've actually taken and facilitated some of these courses over the years, and they have helped me quite a bit. However, the mission of these courses appear to be largely different than mine. My goal is to simply prepare your heart for the techniques you'll learn when you invest in one of those programs.

In other words, what you're about to read is a practical and interesting way to prepare your **heart** for the emotional and spiritual challenges that come with changing your attitude towards budgeting and the handling of money. My hope is that you'll find some practical applications in your life from the wisdom God has hammered into my thick skull over the years. I believe all of my past difficulties were building up to this moment when I'm able to memorialize what He's taught me, so I can pass it on to you. I also believe that if you'll actually apply some of the spiritual approaches to budgeting presented herein, you'll understand the "big picture" of how your attitude towards budgeting actually provides a glimpse into your soul and your overall relationship with Jesus Christ.

The clear intention of this testimony is to also take what I consider to be the most integral part of any solid financial course and put a microscope on it. You see, if you don't learn how to master the spiritual aspects of budgeting, you're actually setting yourself up to fail. Why? Because budgeting is the very heart of your financial life—no matter how much money you make, and no matter if you acknowledge it or not.

Another way to picture this is to think of budgeting as the plug in the bathtub of your finances. You can fill your financial tub with all of the wonderful teachings of some of the financial courses out there, but unless you've mastered the art of budgeting from a _spiritual_ perspective, your plug will inevitably be pulled and your financial life will suffer; possibly draining down the pipes and disappearing. This, of course, would be heartbreaking and a total waste of resources. Because of this danger, budgeting is obviously a very serious subject. But don't worry. I think this book will help.

I feel like what you're about to read can really help you by providing an important perspective from someone who has been through what some might describe as "financial hell" on more than one occasion. My desire is for these previous, bad experiences to provide you with some measure of hope through the honest sharing of the trials and tribulations I've experienced. Admittedly, sharing some of these stumbles is obviously a little embarrassing. But like I said, I hope it will help you in some way. In the end, that would make it all worthwhile. After all, the negative things that happen to us can be turned around by the Lord into a positive testimony if we can help others avoid the same pitfalls.

Although I've written this book from a definitively Christian perspective, my hope is that non-Christians will also be able to glean some tidbits from the simple concepts and practical applications being presented. One of the sections in each chapter is called "Perspectives." I have attempted to delineate biblical teachings from secular thought in some of these sections. While I hope non-Christians will find this book to at least be honest, my real mission is to show true followers of Jesus Christ the importance of following biblical concepts as they grow in their faith and budgeting acuity. I've observed that many Christians will follow Jesus Christ and serve Him on many levels, but will often attempt to leave their wallets on the sidelines during the process. Well, I'm sorry to tell you this, but Jesus wants your _entire_ heart. He doesn't need your money, but He does insist that your whole heart be centered on Him and His kingdom. Anything less is not really an option if you wish to please God.

Since this is my testimony, I'm expressly not presenting these concepts and experiences as a topic for debate. This is a "take it or leave it" book. It's just simply how I see the world of budgeting and the handling of personal finances after having walked through this life for the past five and a half or so decades.

I hope you will benefit greatly from your trip up the daunting mountain of budgeting!

1

Tour Guide

I'm going to go ahead and assume you're reading these words right now for a good reason. I've found that people typically don't like to deal with the subject of budgeting and will actually avoid this topic at all costs. The word "budgeting" itself can summon an enormously negative connotation, and it's almost certainly not in the top one-hundred subjects of discussion at dinner parties.

With that said, let me ask you this—have you asked yourself why you're reading this book? Do you feel obligated to, or do you really want to explore the heart of budgeting? Or, perhaps it's just simple curiosity that's caught your attention. Interestingly, we can sometimes experience an odd sense of inquisitiveness about some of the things we generally avoid or even loathe. Whatever the reason, please don't stop reading until you've at least heard what I have to say. It just may change your heart. This subject certainly changed mine.

I'm going to attempt to dissect the subject of budgeting's inherent negativity issue as we proceed through each chapter. The pessimistic connotations which often accompany our topic of discussion are completely unwarranted. If you wish to live a successful life alongside your money, you simply must push through this "I hate budgeting" baloney and see what's actually going on. I think you'll find that budgeting is really not all that bad. In fact, it has some benefits you may not have previously realized.

Chief among these benefits is that getting on top of the budgeting process can and likely will give you an unexpected sense of accomplishment and peace. At the very minimum, the fear of the unknown will disappear—that is, once you've committed to the entire budgeting process. I've come to believe that you cannot live a successful, God-honoring life on earth if you neglect this simple approach to handling your money in a disciplined and faithful fashion.

For some, budgeting is about overcoming the natural fear of not having enough money to both live your life and provide for your family. For others, it's about finding a way to live with humility. Either way, proper budgeting is an absolutely integral function in not only our financial affairs, but also in our entire life. This is serious business, indeed.

You may be surprised to hear this, but the answer to your financial woes is probably not having more money. I believe that if you'll simply tame your existing money through committed budgeting, you'll effectively quell the nasty beast of discouragement that often swoops in and robs you of joy and attempts to steal your hope. The truth is, if you don't learn to take care of the heart of your financial life—which is exactly what budgeting is—then living a joyful and peaceful life will be virtually impossible in the long run.

As previously mentioned, I believe that what is laid out on these pages can be thought of as a complement and preparatory guide for a more in-depth personal finances program. Although I've presented some of the details of the blueprint I continue to use in my own financial life, a much more comprehensive process is essential as the next step.

The fullness of basic financial planning is resident in these other programs, and it's important for all of us to learn these concepts and techniques. The men and women who have put these various programs together are the true experts. You might think of my purpose for this book as that of a military drill instructor who's hammering away at the basics to hopefully prepare you for what the various financial programs have to offer.

To that end, I believe that once you master the concept of budgeting, you can then master virtually everything else in your financial life. However, if you neglect this simple-but-fundamental function, you'll probably not arrive at, or stay on top of the mountain's summit in your financial life without potentially (or actually) falling off the other side. No, in this scenario, it doesn't necessarily mean you'll lose everything you've ever made if you don't follow a budget. Countless people have made untold fortunes throughout history without one. But none of them have ever taken a penny of it with them when they leave this world.

This is precisely where God enters the picture.

If you diligently tune your budgeting-meter properly, you'll enjoy peace and success, regardless of how much or how little money you make. This is enormously important if you want to enjoy a sense of fearlessness and true contentment in your life—for now, and for the rest of eternity.

That leads me to this basic concept as we begin our journey together. Think of this book as a way for us to climb the difficult mountain of budgeting together. Even the most intrepid mountain explorers typically won't attempt a challenging endeavor like the scaling of Mt. Everest without a proper guide. Neither should you attempt to climb the jagged heights of Mt. Budgeting without an experienced guide. Please allow me to serve you in this way.

Although some people do indeed attempt to go it alone, and even appear to be successful when they reach the summit, if you neglect the spiritual disciplines of basic budgeting, you may not stay on top of your financial mountain. In other words, if you don't master the key components of budgeting that we'll discuss, even the wealthiest people may squander their overall success if they don't learn this basic discipline. And even if they don't squander their wealth here on earth, there's simply no peace if you're not obeying God and honoring Him with your money. Finding eternal peace without God is impossible.

What actually excites me the most about the concept for this book is that I feel like it's applicable to most everyone. This includes those who make $10K per year and those who make $10 million per year—as well as everyone in-between. Many of us who aren't wealthy often feel that having the influx of a bunch of cash will solve all of the problems in our life. This, of course, is incorrect on many levels. Without the moderating "plug" of budgeting in our personal financial bathtub, it's possible to make millions of dollars, only to have it disappear down the drain where you'll be left feeling cold and empty. Even if you don't end up broke, you'll be left spiritually lacking if you don't honor God with your money.

On the other hand, once you've fully mastered the art and discipline of personal budgeting, you'll be absolutely amazed at how much peace and contentment that can descend upon your entire life. I believe that many wealthy people who don't commit to budgeting are, at the very minimum, constantly worried about losing their wealth. But when you have your hands wrapped around every single penny in your financial life, and those pennies are used appropriately, balanced, and in honor of Jesus Christ, an amazing calmness accompanies it. This true serenity in your soul only happens if you're glorifying God with your money, not when you're being self-centered with it.

Speaking of that, if you've been either intentionally or unwittingly building a financial Tower of Babel to yourself with your money, you're essentially only glorifying you. This is a deal buster in God's kingdom. There is only one God, and it's not any one of us.

Interestingly, for those who have very little money, these same budgeting concepts apply to those who have a substantial bank account. The techniques and approach don't change. The only thing that changes is the scale of what you manage.

Listen … it is one thing to be broke, but it's quite another to be broke and not know it. Why? Because fear of the unknown creates a world where potential financial marauders always seem to be circling around you with a death stare. I've found that it's much easier to deal with these villains (like needing a new roof, a car that's dying, or enormous hospital bills) when we know who they are and what they look like. When we don't quantify these potential or real financial enemies, they always end up looming as specters of potential tragedy in our financial lives. To my way of thinking, having to deal with a dark forest of financial unknowns is very uncomfortable. I'd much rather quantify my situation, even if it's bad, than to wonder what's bothering me and not know why.

So whether you're wealthy and feel poor; or whether you're poor and feel a strangling hopelessness; or whether you're somewhere in-between these polar opposite situations, the mastery of budgeting will plant your feet on the ground and give you a sense of serenity which can revolutionize your financial life. And that, my friends, is why you should finish reading this book.

Like I said, I'd like for you to think of me as your tour guide (and sometimes drill instructor) as we climb this mountain together. I promise to be as transparent as I possibly can be as we conquer the heights of this budgeting-thing. When you hear of some of the experiences I've walked through, it just may give you the confidence that your tour guide is in this to protect you from making the same mistakes. After all, it's not about how many times you stumble. It's about how many times you get back on your feet after being knocked down.

Perspectives

Let's start off this section with some truth.

Those who love Jesus Christ and have surrendered their life to God cannot logically hold back on also surrendering their finances to Him. I'll go more in-depth into this subject in later chapters, but the Christian perspective demands following the example of Christ, who talked more about money than just about anything else. No, He didn't do this because God needs our money. Instead, He demands our hearts. God actually has all of the money, and He knows how dangerous the love of money is. We cannot love and serve money more than God or it becomes false idol worship. In all of my biblical studies, I can tell you with confidence, the Lord will not allow idols to come between each of His forgiven children and Himself. Idol worship is for pagans, not Christians.

How we approach the concept of budgeting is often indicative of the big picture of what we really think about God. Why? Because obedience is the hallmark of the Christian life. It's about dethroning ourselves and submitting to our Father. It's about our faith in Him. It's not about us. This perspective stands in stark contrast to the secular world, which seems to lean heavily towards fulfilling personal goals and desires. While these things can certainly be important, everyone must remember that we all came into this life kicking and screaming, and we'll leave this life essentially doing the same thing. In other words, death is real to both the believer and the non-believer. Believers must have faith or it is impossible to please God (*see Hebrews 11:6*). Non-believers generally feel they must personally accomplish everything they can during this life because there's nothing after it. Or at best, they don't feel like they can really know what happens after we die, so they'd better hurry up and accomplish their goals. While I certainly disagree with the contention of naturalists who believe there is no life after this one, and therefore there is no judgment of sin, my concern lies elsewhere.

It lies with my fellow believers.

What I find to be a totally incongruent attitude towards basic biblical principles is when someone identifies themself as a follower of Jesus Christ and claims to love Him, but one who also conducts themself in the ways of the world—especially when it comes to finances. These days, as best as I can tell, the ways of the world tend to glorify each person's "bucket list." To a world without God, a bucket list must be completed during each person's time on earth before they "kick the bucket."

I can certainly understand why an unbeliever would feel this way. It's actually a logical reaction to their worldview. However, I don't understand at all how someone can claim to believe in God's promises of heaven and the new earth, but who lives like they're not going to actually be there one day. If you have faith, you must demonstrate it to both God and to the world. A Christian cannot believe in God's promises of heaven and not conduct themself in a way which demonstrates this belief.

That just doesn't make any sense.

For the Christian, budgeting is a faith issue, to be sure. Essentially, I believe that how you budget your money (if at all), and your attitude towards it, very much demonstrates your faith (or lack thereof) in God's promises of eternal life beyond this one. In other words, how you view your wallet and what you want to do with it often depicts exactly where your focus in life and faith in God is. Far too often, we can feel that we believe in and love Jesus Christ, but our actions must match our beliefs. You cannot have it both ways. Either the world is right, or God is right.

➢ My Story

I was always a pretty good student in school and during my illustrious year of college. During my education, I was much better at English, history, and the sciences, than math. Although I was pretty good at basic math, the advanced subjects like trigonometry, etc., were beyond me. The good news is that you don't need to be good at advanced mathematical subjects to master the basic debits and credits associated with good budgeting. It's about execution and commitment, not complication or education.

Sadly, like it is for most people, handling money wasn't a natural talent for me. When I opened my first checking account right after high school, I actually bounced my first check. So yeah, you're reading a budgeting book written by a person who was a total numbskull when it comes to basic finances when I was younger. Because of this, I hope you can see there's hope for nearly everyone.

I've found that the mastering of basic budgeting techniques is very much a learned talent, not a natural one. How you view something as simple as budgeting demonstrates in simple black and white terms just where your focus in life is. Far too often, our focus is on our self and our goals, not on God and His eternal kingdom. Like I said, the world teaches us to focus on fulfilling our own dreams and goals before we die.

That philosophy basically gives someone a blank check to do whatever they want to do with their money.

On the other hand, the Lord teaches us to focus on Jesus Christ and our eternal life with Him. This stands in stark contrast to the world's approach to budgeting and money. I don't believe you can live a successful life of faith in Jesus unless you do things His way. This was a hard lesson for me to learn.

I can assure you, if God can take a "regular dude" like me and show me how to honor Him with how I approach budgeting, He can and will do it for you, also. As mentioned, I see budgeting as a matter of faith. It's also a matter of the will. Budgeting is not anything beyond the ability for a regular person to accomplish. How I handled money when I entered the adult world indicated exactly where my heart was—in the world. Thank God He eventually showed me the way out of it. He will also do the same thing for you.

While it took me many years to discover all of this, it doesn't have to be that way for you. In fact, I very much hope this book will help you to <u>want</u> to do things differently. If you desire a different result than what you've already experienced, you absolutely must change things up. Truthfully, if you really love the Lord, you'll absolutely want to change things up and honor Him with your money. One way or another, God is going to teach you His way of doing things. You might as well commit to doing it now. The adjustments you make in your financial life can and will bring you and your family much more joy and peace than you can possibly imagine. Honoring God always brings peace. Focusing on and honoring the world does just the opposite.

➤ RYB, Dude!

For those who have read any of my scripture-based novels, you know that I like to teach basic biblical concepts through various types of stories and parables. The "RYB, Dude!" is a reference to "Read Your Bible." It's a catch phrase used by the fictional protagonist in my books, an affable angel named Mick. In each chapter, I'll highlight its essential concepts with a verse or verses in this section.

Yes, using ample amounts of scripture may be a unique approach to writing novels, but it's what God led me to do. The one thing I wanted to do for this book, however, was to only utilize specific verses for each chapter so I could really concentrate on the concepts and not turn this whole thing into a long sermon. So for those who are biblically inclined, I've included some specific verse references for you to follow up on if you so desire.

Personally speaking, I largely use Biblegateway.com and review several different biblical translations when doing research for my books or a bible study. Right up front, please know that I will expressly not be delving into any of the arguments about which translation is better than another. Jesus Christ is the center of my faith, and I hope that many fellow believers will read this book and be blessed by it. I'm also hoping that open-minded non-believers and/or spiritual seekers will also read this book.

To that end, I'm stating my specific biblical citations using both the King James Version (KJV) and New International Version (NIV). Those who read each of these specific translations typically dislike the other one. For the sake of unity within the body of Christ, I'm using both. I'll ask for both sides of the issue to tolerate the presence of the other translation as you read along. This book is about Jesus Christ and His glory, not arguing over which translation to use.

For this chapter, I'd like you to consider a verse I mentioned a moment ago. I often think of its meaning and remind myself of its importance. I also like to share it with others when we're doing a bible study. This verse is a wonderful "big picture" concept I tend to focus on in my own walk of faith. In fact, I think every single follower of Christ should pin this verse up in a conspicuous area and read it daily:

Hebrews 11:6:

KJV ... "But without faith it is impossible to please him: for he that cometh to God must believe that he is, and that he is a rewarder of them that diligently seek him."

NIV ... "And without faith it is impossible to please God, because anyone who comes to him must believe that he exists and that he rewards those who earnestly seek him."

As we climb the mountain of budgeting together, we need to remember that if we don't have faith in God and His ways, it is impossible to please Him. So let me ask you this: How's your faith doing these days? Does the budgeting of your money actually reflect how you really feel about Jesus Christ—just as I'm proposing? If you think I'm wrong about that, what's your reasoning?

➢ Actions

So you're a chapter into this book and you can see how's it's laid out. At this point, the best course of action is to determine that you're going to finish this entire thing with me operating as your tour guide. Budgeting is not a subject people typically want to talk about, but it's absolutely essential to both your life <u>and</u> your faith.

We're at the bottom of the mountain right now, in what you might call a type of "base camp." We have a long way to go to reach the summit, so I challenge you to stay with me as we break camp and begin our march upwards. I really think you'll learn a few things along the way, and perhaps even have a chuckle or two. More importantly, I hope you'll see the glory of God contained within these pages. I've gone through a lot of financial pain in my life. I truly hope you don't have to, as well.

Like I've said, budgeting isn't the most popular subject, but it's very important. Let's do this together.

➢ Let's Whiteboard That

This section is for a topical parting shot or shots to leave you with at the end of each chapter. I really enjoy whiteboards for two primary reasons: (1) they're excellent visual depictions of simple ideas being described and/or presented; and (2) they're fantastic for hard hitting quotes or sayings that make a salient point. This section is intended to use various quotes to provide a kind of synopsis of what you've just read. So for the first one, here goes:

> "What is right is not always
> popular,
> and what is popular is not always
> right."
> **Albert Einstein**

2

Open Mind

As we exit base camp at the bottom of Mt. Budgeting, I think it's important for you to take a moment and open your mind to all of the possibilities of what you'll be encountering during our journey. In all honesty, not everything we'll discuss during our time together will seem all that pleasant—at least, at first it may not. However, understanding these concepts is nonetheless important for you to find true budgeting success. So let's soldier-up and move ahead.

Any adept guide will always be honest and transparent with those who are entrusted to his or her care. For our voyage, I must be brutally honest with you because I want to help you avoid falling off the side of the mountain—back into a non- or minimal budgeting chasm of frustration. Please believe me; it's for your own safety that I'm telling you these things. The transparency will come into play when I'm sharing some of the stumbles I've encountered during my past trek towards committed budgeting and its resulting serenity in my life.

If dealing with a budget has been a negative subject for you, I get that. I really do. But I also greatly desire for you to find the same peace I've fought so hard to attain. Living righteously and within one's means has a ripple effect throughout your entire life. It definitely has a wonderful windfall for your body, mind, and soul. Living in a financially undisciplined fashion has just the opposite effect. It can wreak havoc on your life if you don't do something about it.

Finding contentment in your budgeting life is probably going to entail some changes. If you don't actually amend how you do things now, how can you expect to experience any positive changes later? With that in mind, the most important thing I need to tell you at this point is that Jesus Christ is king.

Yeah, we've all heard that before, and many of us have nodded our heads when we hear this statement. But is Jesus <u>really</u> the king of your life? In the past, I have viewed (as most of us have at one time or another), that God is essentially a type of "cosmic Santa Claus" who is obligated to provide me with everything I want in life. Does this expectation sound silly to you? It sure does to me. Based on a lot of experience and self-reflection, what feels absolutely awful to me now is the fact that deep within the trenches of my heart, that's the way I used to think about God. And if you're being honest, you've probably done the same thing—or perhaps you still do. So ... please consider this statement:

> In the sinful, self-centered
> human heart, the motivation
> behind chasing after money is
> almost always about control.

That's why just hearing the word "budget" makes so many of us recoil with distaste, fear, and/or out-and-out disgust. Why? Because creating and adhering to a budget means you can't do everything you want to do. The result of not being able to do whatever you desire means you have to submit to someone or something other than yourself. From the humanistic perspective, that means we're not in total control. It means we cannot indulge ourselves however we want. To the sinful human spirit, this is as unpleasant as it is painful. At least, at first it is. But that can change.

In fact, it <u>should</u> change.

The bible teaches us that we're all born under the sinful curse of Adam, and that we, as his descendants, must overcome our propensity to rule over our own life as the god of our own world. If you really think about it, don't we worry about money because we feel like having it prevents us from living what we would consider to be a lesser life? Don't we feel that having a certain amount of money means we'll be able to maintain our current way of living and/or ascend to living the lifestyle of our dreams?

Of course we feel that way—naturally, that is. But that's not all there is to the story.

When you drill just below the surface of our desire for money, in virtually all cases, it's not hard to find some cleverly disguised pride. Believe me when I tell you, although I've submitted my life to serving Jesus Christ, the human tendency to worry about how much money we have—which in my own mind keeps me from getting booted out on the street—is largely terrifying in nature. I believe this is a particularly acute condition in the United States, which has so many available commodities which can help to enhance our lifestyles with all sorts of comfort.

Digging down further, I believe we have a stigma in our culture about failing. This stigma is as silent as it is lethal to the soul. Personally speaking, I can only soothe my worries about money when my spiritual sense kicks in and reminds me that God is my complete provider. For me, to not trust God for any of my provision and to take this daunting responsibility on myself is akin to seeking my own godship. And that, my friends, is the ultimate deal buster in God's kingdom. *Exodus 20:3* gives us the first commandment, which tells us there can only be one God in this world. That means we can't have any other gods before Him—including ourselves. This also includes our unhealthy love of money. Check that. It <u>especially</u> includes our sinful love of money. I believe that an obsession with money often reflects a low level of faith.

So as we begin our initial ascent, please keep in mind that no matter how much you may want it to be otherwise (and I totally get that), this world belongs to Jesus Christ. We can either be a part of His eternal kingdom by loving and serving Him, or we can go it alone and do things our own way until the day we die. Although it's difficult for the human mind to comprehend how we can have the freedom to choose, yet God is still all-knowing, that doesn't change the truth of this basic biblical fact. In other words, arguing about the truth has no effect on the truth itself. And Jesus Christ is the Truth. He is the only way.

Essentially, in order to forge ahead successfully, I'm asking you to please keep an open mind. If you're reading this book out of obligation or compulsion, you'll likely not have the proper mind-set to receive the concepts we're going to cover. Also, if you really hate God or totally deny that He exists, you probably aren't going to like what I have to say, either.

Anyway, believer or not, if you'll simply allow for the possibility that God exists, and that He isn't here to shower you with whatever you want in life, and that how we treat our money is initially like trying to tame a wild beast that always wants its way, I think you'll be embarking on our journey with the right attitude and an appropriately open mind. Having an open mind will undoubtedly help to contribute towards a positive mind set for our journey as we make our way towards the mountain's summit.

On the other hand, if you don't want to maintain an open mind during our journey, you're leaving base camp with the wrong attitude and are probably just wasting your time. I don't know about you, but I detest wasting my time because it's such a valuable commodity. I'm sorry for the truth-bomb, but I just had to say it before we proceeded any further.

➤ Perspectives

Okay, so this bucket list concept has definitely landed smack-dab in the middle of our modern lexicon, and it seems to be here to stay. Because of that, here is what I have to say about bucket lists.

If you are a true follower of Jesus Christ, you cannot possibly want to complete your bucket list before you die. To feel the pressure that your life will not be fulfilled in some way if you don't hurry up and accomplish certain desires is the default view that many naturalists maintain. As I see it, a naturalist believes there is no life beyond our physical existence, so everything you are and everything you do resides within our physical existence here on earth. In other words, if you don't live it up now, you never will.

I respectfully disagree.

If you identify as a Christian, I'd like you to consider the importance of the focal point of our "family business." If you read any of the gospels, you'll see that Jesus didn't come to serve, but to suffer and die for others. Far too often, I don't think we consider the importance of Christ's forty days on earth, post-resurrection, but pre-ascension. In this state, Jesus appeared and disappeared, ate food with his disciples, demonstrated that he was "flesh and bone," and even walked through a wall. While it's true that only Jesus is fully glorified at this time, it's also true that His followers will all continue in this same path one day. The bible refers to Jesus as the "first fruits." When you think about the enormity of the universe and the possibilities of God's redemption of it, it's easy to get excited about all of the wonderful things we'll likely do for the rest of eternity as we follow in the steps of our King.

When we look up at the stars on a clear night, we can all see there's a lot of space out there in the universe. It doesn't take a doctorate in astronomy from MIT to see just how vast our universe is. But have you ever wondered why the universe is so immense? Here's the concept I'd like you to consider ... I believe my true bucket list won't even begin to be fulfilled until I pass from this world. With God's incredible promises of heaven and the new earth in mind, it seems to me that it's much easier to submit to Him during our short stay on this rock. That is, it's easier to follow God's will if one really believes in God's promises.

I most certainly do.

Oftentimes, my mind wanders off and I think about all of the incredible things in store for myself and my fellow followers of Christ. There's a lot of space out there in the universe, and I believe God will refill it one day with awe inspiring places and things for his redeemed children. The possibilities are absolutely endless. With that in mind, I hope you'll consider opening your mind to the possibilities of what may happen after a follower of Christ's stay on earth is complete. From the humanistic perspective, it's virtually impossible to do everything you want to do before you die. But for the Christian, have you ever considered what you may do <u>after</u> you die?

Without question, God's kingdom is both vast and wonderful. However, we're only seeing the fallen version of it right now. There's a redeemed universe awaiting all of those who love and believe in Jesus Christ. When you embrace the fullness of our future without the hindrance of the pain and suffering we currently experience here on earth, it's easy to get excited about the future. <u>Very</u> excited.

So while you're still here in this fallen world with all of its limitations and pitfalls, you'll need a good plug for your financial bathtub, which is your budget. A proper budget should serve as a physical, mental, and spiritual guardian in your life. As previously stated, I believe that how you manage your budget demonstrates to God exactly where your focus in life is.

Let me ask you a question. If God was to examine your personal checkbook right now, what would He see? Would He see what is truly important to you? To me, I don't want to be embarrassed when I meet Jesus in-person one day, so I strive to offer my monthly budget to the Lord as an offering at His altar. It may not be all that I want it to be right now, but I can tell you with confidence that all of my heart is in it. I very much strive to please God with our budget. This is very much an ongoing process.

I languished in life for a few years after graduation from high school in 1979. I had no direction and no idea what to do. After a few lousy jobs and about a year of college, I landed in the trucking industry back in 1982—almost by accident. I'm happy to say, I continue to work in this wonderful business and have met some incredible people through this vocation. Although I've thoroughly enjoyed working in the trucking industry, I honestly had no idea how much God would ultimately bless me through it. I was a mere twenty years old when I started into the business, and at that time, I knew very little about life. Throughout the three and half-plus decades in it, God has been molding and shaping me all along the way. Of course, I was completely oblivious to this process until I began writing books back in 2009.

As I reflect back, most of the duties during my time in the trucking business have always included working with basic numbers. Starting in 1982, I worked for five-plus years in pricing, then four years in billing, then six years in training and contract administration, and finally, twenty-plus years in sales and recruiting. Working with numbers has always been a huge part of my daily work activities.

Why do I tell you this?

It's because every single thing I've done during my working career has included the utilization of how to measure basic dollars and cents. This includes the application of rates all the way to the generation and tracking of revenue growth. Crunching numbers has long since been hammered into my work life, and it has ultimately benefited my budgeting life, to be sure.

Essentially, I'm saying that you don't need to be an Einstein when it comes to mathematics in order to be an effective budgeter. If I can do it, most everyone can do it. With all of that said, please consider this. I feel that good budgeting is all about:

> Commitment—not complication
>
> Execution—not education
>
> The crucifixion—not our
> gratification

If you possess any level of common sense, then budgeting can become a tremendous asset for you—not the liability it so often is. Budgetarily (is that a word?) speaking, commitment and a pure heart are more important than aptitude. One can have all of the mathematical acuity in the world, but if you don't respect and submit to the boundaries of a budget, you won't be able to please God with your money. Unfortunately, this can and often does affect your entire relationship with the creator of all things. Budgeting is obviously critically important. If it wasn't, I certainly wouldn't have spent all of this time writing a book about it.

➤ RYB, Dude!

Hebrews 13:5:

KJV ... "Let your conversation be without covetousness; and be content with such things as ye have: for he hath said, I will never leave thee, nor forsake thee."

NIV ... "Keep your lives free from the love of money and be content with what you have, because God has said, 'Never will I leave you; never will I forsake you.'"

➤ Actions

Please be open to the possibility that you may not achieve all of your wildest dreams and goals during your brief stay here on this pretty blue rock called earth. Although most of us do indeed have a real bucket list of some sort, God may not want you to experience all of it before He brings you into His presence in heaven, and ultimately on the new earth. Helping to encourage others to join you as a follower of Jesus Christ is more important to God than any of us fulfilling our personal desires during this brief part of our existence. To be a successful disciple—which is exactly what <u>all</u> followers of Christ are called to be—means you'll need to sacrifice some of your current desires to ensure success in what we're called to be, which is ambassadors of the gospel. The Greek word for sacrificial love used in the bible is "agape" love. If God sacrificed His only son for our sins, can you see your way to sacrificing some of your current personal desires to honor and serve His kingdom?

With all of that said, to ensure success during our brief time together, I encourage you to work hard at keeping an open mind (and open bible) and realize that the earth as it now stands is only a brief weigh station before entering eternity. More importantly, what you do or do not attain or achieve here on earth now, can and probably will be redeemed by Jesus Christ when the prophecies are fulfilled and He ushers in the eternal state of the world. Far too often, we think of heaven as an endless festival of harp playing and hymn singing. That, my friends, is unbiblical baloney. Being with Jesus is so much more than engaging in an eternal church service. Jesus carries the title of "Immanuel," which means "God with us," or "God among us." That's an amazing concept when you really think about it. In biblical Christianity, you don't have to work your way to heaven—Jesus has done the work for you. Having a <u>saving</u> relationship with Jesus Christ is the most important thing in the world.

But all good relationships also have responsibilities.

Scripture tells us that true believers will not only go to heaven to be with Jesus when we die, but that heaven will be moved back to earth one day (see *Revelation 21:1-4*). This promise is rock solid and we can absolutely count on it. Why? Because in every case where there's been a past biblical prophecy, there's also been a one-hundred percent fulfillment rate. If you ask me, that's pretty darned good. That's something we can absolutely count on for future biblical prophecies. In other words, previously fulfilled prophecies should give us great confidence in all of God's future prophecies to be fulfilled one day.

When you fully embrace the biblical assurance that your life in God's presence will be sorrow-free one day, your attitude towards lassoing your finances into a budget becomes much more palatable and comfortable to live with. When you fully embrace the role God has called you to fulfill, which is one of being a disciple, your fear of not having enough money to live your life will become less important. When you realize the fact that God thinks of you as a valued son or daughter in His kingdom, your view of life and attitude towards it changes. Your life actually becomes immeasurably better and much more satisfying. You realize you're not alone because God didn't create you to be that way. However, you must love God to become a part of the perfect world that awaits true Christians.

Essentially, I'm saying that if you love Jesus Christ and have surrendered your life to Him, you need to just relax. The events in your life will unfold as God sees fit. Whatever you don't receive on earth right now is something He just may want to shower upon you one day in heaven or later, on the new earth. God has promised believers the glory of eternity one day, and that's good enough for me. By the time you finish this book, I hope you'll feel the same way.

If you don't know God through Jesus Christ, please consider surrendering your heart to Him right now. God wants you to be fulfilled in Him more than anything else. Once you become a member of God's family, you become a son or daughter of the Creator of all things.

That's a really, really, big deal.

➢ Let's Whiteboard That

"The condition of an
enlightened mind is a
surrendered heart."
Alan Redpath

3

Wild Stallion

Most everyone needs some form of transportation to get from one point to another, or to travel great distances without having to walk on your own two feet. Today, we have wonderful automobiles to get us from one point to another. There are also many other options, like planes, buses, and trains, etc., to get the job done. Through advancing technology, we can even order a car ride from our smart phone and watch the driver pull up to our exact spot. All of these modern conveniences are wonderful, indeed.

But let's hearken back to a bygone era for just a moment. Back in the old west, they primarily used horses for transportation. That's what I'd like you to think about for this part of our journey. You see, horses were quite powerful and perhaps even enjoyable to ride, but they weren't born with the ability to immediately take on riders. They had to be trained to do so. Absent of proper training, a horse could not possibly serve its master. In its natural state, a horse was wild, unpredictable, and dangerous.

They still are.

Back then, as in today, it took great skill and effort to take a wild stallion and train it to be a loyal steed. A skilled hand had to break the wild horse down and train it to work for its master. Without this training, a wild horse could drag an unsuspecting rider off the trail and into the wilderness. At that point, the horse could actually do whatever it wanted to do. It had a will of its own and it answered to no one. But it was vulnerable. It had no protector. Savage predators could take the horse down and nothing could stop them from being eaten. Although they were untamed at heart, a wild horse's bigger purpose was to be trained to serve and sometimes save their master. When a horse was trained to serve instead of wandering aimlessly, it was noble. It had purpose. It was obedient and lived a better life. It served God's purpose to help mankind.

The same concept applies to your budget.

In its natural, untamed state, your budget is wild at heart and has a will of its own. It is hedonistic and self-serving. It only seeks to glorify itself in the moment and cannot and will not serve you or save you. It cannot travel distances with you because it has no purpose or sense of direction. It is wild, wooly, and dangerous. Because of this, to make a budget viable, it must be tamed and brought into submission. In the ongoing battle between you and your budget, there is no quarter. It is a zero-sum game. There is a winner and there is a loser. The question is, what do you want it to be? You are very much in control of your budget—that is, if you decide to be.

In many cases, when we begin our working life, our spending habits are very much like the wild stallion, which has an independent and strong will of its own. The stallion doesn't want to be tamed. It thinks it's designed to run around on its own. It thinks it should go wherever it wants to go. But how can it serve any productive purpose if it merely runs around and follows its cavalier impulses?

It can't.

Let's admit something. We all love serving ourselves. It's our natural state. If you don't follow Jesus Christ (and I pray that you do, or will), then you probably don't see the need to have your "wild stallion" tendencies towards money and budgeting be brought into submission to

God. That only makes sense. But in my opinion, obedient budgeting for the Christian is an outward act of worship towards God. If this is true (it is), then followers of Christ should take budgeting very seriously.

For those who love Jesus Christ, I beg you to consider just how easily money can become a false idol in your life. Without proper taming, your budget is your enemy. It hates your guts and you may not even know it. But with just a little bit of training, your budget can absolutely become your best friend. It will guide you closer to Christ as well as serving your life and your family well.

Asset or foe? Your budget follows your direction. It will undoubtedly wander off aimlessly until it's trained to do differently. Your budget has the ability to serve you, but only if you commit to the process. That's essentially why we're climbing this mountain together. Don't feel badly if your budget is still a wild stallion—that's the natural state for all of us.

On the other hand, <u>do</u> feel badly if you want your budget to remain a wild stallion. I'm not talking about feeling guilty. I'm talking about keeping an open mind and acknowledging that your wild stallion is working against you—when it should be working for you. There's some training to be done to overcome this, so let's get to the process of taming your wild budgeting beast.

➤ Perspectives

For the Christian, if you don't recognize that mankind is born sinful and in desperate need for Jesus to forgive our sins, then I'm not sure you're getting the whole purpose of why Christ died on the cross. When you examine sin's impact on the biblical text, you'll see an amazing fact: exactly two chapters in the bible are about mankind before sin entered the world (*Genesis 1 and 2*), and two chapters are about mankind after Jesus has dealt with and put away evil and sin once and for all. When that happens, Christians enter the eternal state (see *Revelation 21 and 22*). Without sin entering the world through our ancestors Adam and Eve, we wouldn't be having this discussion right now. But because of it, our thoughts and attitudes towards money are naturally flawed and sinful. They absolutely must be tamed.

The non-Christian perspective on budgeting can vary greatly, but a naturalist who doesn't believe in the afterlife will generally look at life on earth under a completely different lens than a follower of Christ. If you don't believe in God and feel like there's no life beyond this one, you'll probably not see your budget as being wild at all. At the very minimum, you'll certainly not see your budget as something that needs the involvement of a God who you don't believe in. A naturalist will generally see their budget as the means to feed their own, personal focus in life, and it absolutely must do its job before their death.

I say all of this to point out that a Christian's perspective on budgeting is logically different than a non-believer.

That isn't to say that someone who doesn't believe in God cannot live a good life of proper budgeting and helping others. Interestingly, many non-believers often do. However, that's not the point. Our first commandment as Christians is to love God with all of our heart and soul, and the second one is like it—to love our neighbor as our self. In God's world, you can't do just one of these commandments. You have to do both.

So let me get back to something we touched on earlier. If we were to examine your budget right now, would we see God and others being loved, or would we see our self being loved, served, and exalted? The answer to this question will demonstrate exactly where you stand right now. If you actually have a budget, it's staring right at you, in black and white. You may not like the answer to the question of who is being served by your budget, but a budget doesn't lie. Whether you're rich or you're poor, or anywhere in-between, your budget demonstrates exactly where your focus in life is.

➢ My Story

Growing up, I had some fairly bad experiences in my religious life with different churches and different denominations. Actually, these bad experiences happened from the time I was a kid until I was in my forties. It was then that I finally began the process of understanding exactly who Jesus Christ really is. All it took for this spiritual awakening was a simple invite from a customer who asked us to join him one Sunday at his church. God handled the rest. That was back in 2004, and at that time, I began a wonderful quest to truly know the Lord. It has been an absolutely amazing journey ever since.

After my mom passed away a few years later in 2008, I started writing scripture-based evangelical novels the following year. This was largely an attempt to deal with my grief and to help keep my eyes focused forward, into God's eternal kingdom. As I studied the bible and wrote my books over the years, I found some amazingly simple biblical concepts. Those simple concepts are very much a part of this book.

Anyway, there's a lot more details to it, but it was in 2006 that everything began to change for me—biblically speaking, that is. It was then that I read the book "Heaven" by Randy Alcorn. The biblical concepts presented in that book absolutely changed my entire spiritual life. It was only after seeing what God actually has to say about our temporary pain on earth and what is to follow for those who love Him that everything about Jesus began to really make sense to me. Essentially, my entire spiritual perspective began to evolve from that day forward. Actually, it continues to evolve, every single day. The bible calls this "sanctification." The basic concept of sanctification comes into play after we have surrendered our life to Jesus Christ. At that point, God begins to mold each of His children into the image of His son.

I truly thank God that He's led me to share my story with you. There have been many bumps along the way, but here I am. I can't believe He has taken an ordinary dude like me and shown me how to serve His kingdom by sharing this testimony. My hope is that as all of you grow in your faith, God will also use your story to help encourage others. After all, everyone has a story to tell. When you think about it, negative experiences can become positive ones when they're later used to help encourage your neighbor. That's exactly what I'm attempting to do with this book.

Perhaps one day, you'll be able to use your testimony in a similar way.

➤ RYB, Dude!

Luke 16:10:

KJV ... "He that is faithful in that which is least is faithful also in much: and he that is unjust in the least is unjust also in much."

NIV ... "Whoever can be trusted with very little can also be trusted with much, and whoever is dishonest with very little will also be dishonest with much."

As we notice our base camp at the bottom of the mountain begin to fade in the distance below, we need to press in and continue to examine our thoughts and feelings about budgeting as we move ahead. So let me ask you a question—is your mind open to budgeting with God's kingdom as your primary focus? Are you willing to tame your wild stallion and turn it into a loyal, life-saving servant of God's plan for your life? If so, please continue to look in the mirror as we examine the budgeting process from all of the physical, mental, and spiritual aspects. Unfortunately, there is no magic bullet here. This journey up the mountain is about you. It's about being honest and examining your inner thoughts and feelings. It's about your spiritual progress. The physical things in life follow the spiritual; not the opposite.

If you're still on the pathway up the mountain with me, at this point, you probably understand that you need to make some changes. If you haven't bailed on me yet, you probably acknowledge the "wild" element to how you've approached your financial boundaries thus far in life. If you continue this process, your comfort level with what's happening to your view of budgeting will likely continue to grow and evolve—just like it did for me. I promise you, it will ultimately bring you peace if you keep trekking up the sometimes arduous spiritual incline. The journey may feel a bit difficult at times, but it really isn't when you look back on it. It's absolutely not difficult when you discover what's waiting for you at the summit. Or rather, who is waiting for you at the summit (hint, it's Jesus).

Our journey together is an absolutely necessary endeavor for many people, so you're not alone if this is your situation. Once you've reached the summit, your pain will hopefully have turned into some level of comfort due to your budget being within God's will. With that in mind, please continue your ascent. Sooner or later, you're going to need to overcome your hidden financial fears and find solace in your financial dealings.

Let's face it. The older you get, the harder it is to deal with stress. The Lord awaits all of us to surrender our will to Him, every single day. Don't hold onto what may seem comfortable at this moment. Step out in faith and allow God to remove your selfish desires. As one who previously lived only for me, I can tell you with confidence that by allowing God to tame my naturally wild stallion tendencies, many of my fears in life have ultimately disappeared. Or at the very least, they've been greatly diminished.

I have one more suggestion. Please quit thinking about winning the lottery. Yes, we've all pretty much joked about "I'd do this or that" if we won the lottery. But this is a rare occurrence indeed (more on this later). The danger in indulging those thoughts is that they can and often do become a false reality in our soul because they slowly morph into a false sanctuary of hope. The spiritual problem with the thought of winning the lottery is that it can provide a false hope that will almost always end in disappointment. I suggest you stop thinking about how awesome it would be to discover the winning lottery ticket, and instead realize that if you love Jesus Christ, you've already won the lottery.

Big time.

For those few who have actually won a bunch of cash in a lottery, I say congratulations. I hope you'll read this book and apply the same basic principles as the one who makes very little money. A budget is about submission and sacrifice. It's a vision you must keep your focus centered on. A proper budget is noble, no matter how much money you make.

The other problem I've found with the "I need to win the lottery" mindset is that it can promote a Superman mentality. Now what I mean by that is, far too often, we think about all of the good we can do if we won a lottery. Personally speaking, I've thought about all of the family, friends, and charities I could help if I won a gazillion dollars with the winning ticket. The problem with that mind-set is that I actually wanted to be Superman so I could save everyone. Well … we already have a Superman who can save the world. His name is Jesus Christ. That's His job, not mine. It's also not your job, so I suggest you stop thinking about it. Back in 2014, I bought my last lottery ticket. I have no plans to ever buy another one.

Anyway, God loves you. You need to love Him back by doing the uncomfortable thing and honor Him by joyfully submitting to and taming your budget. Allow God to bless you again and again by taking care of what money you do have. After all, why would He entrust you with more if you're not being faithful with less?

> ➤ **Let's Whiteboard That**

"Disobedience to conscience makes conscience blind."
C.S. Lewis

"One act of obedience is better than one hundred sermons."
Dietrich Bonhoeffer

4

Open Heart

Let's go ahead talk about your heart. It's a pretty important subject.

First off, let me say something quite obvious. Your heart is the center of your physical body. Every drop of your blood passes through it. Continuously. The heart is an incredibly strong muscle because it has to be. Effective muscles are designed to be exercised often so they can remain viable and healthy enough to do their job. Even though we don't often think about our beating heart as we conduct our day-to-day activities, we would certainly know if something was wrong with it. In fact, if your heart wasn't at the center of your body, nothing would happen. You wouldn't survive. If you look at someone's physical body on the outside, you wouldn't necessarily know if it had a beating heart or not. There may be evidence something is in there pumping away, but not hard proof. Generally speaking, you can only see a beating heart if your body is opened up.

Okay, maybe that's a little gross. Let's move on.

My point is, whether you believe it or not, the same concept is true of your budget. It's the very heart of your financial life. Every penny you have flows through it—or at least, it should. Even if you have lots and lots of money, if all of it flows through a properly balanced budget, your spiritual health will remain strong and it will likely grow.

But some of us don't have a formalized budget. I get that. That's why I'm here—to convince you to commit to and maintain one. The reality of your budget serving as the beating heart of your financial life is nonetheless true, even if you don't acknowledge it. Your budgetary heart is actually there, even if you don't see it right now. The problem lies with the fact that with so many of us, we haven't been formally introduced to our budget. I really think it's time to fix that. Your budgeting heart is in there beating away; you just may not know what it looks like yet.

What I'm driving at is simply this—now is the time to open up your financial body and let's see how your budget's heart is beating. You see, every single time you pay a bill, make a charge on a debit or credit card, deposit a paycheck into your checking account, or virtually any other monetary transaction, you're working with your budget. Your budget serves you by performing its duties, even though you may not have acknowledged him or her.

Yes, you heard me right. I just personified your budget from "it" to "him" or "her." This, of course, was intentional. Since I'm a male, I refer to my budget as "him." You can go ahead and drop a name on your budget if you like (no foul language, please—that's counterproductive). For a later chapter, this will all end up making much more sense. Please stay with me. I promise I haven't gone off the deep end.

At least, not yet.

I'm well aware that some of you who are reading this book already have a budget to guide your financial life. To you, I say—*bravo*. Well done. On the other hand, it always surprises me just how many people don't formalize their budget. I'm not saying those who fall into this category (I used to be one) are bad people. And I'm not saying that the lack of a budget makes one bad at managing money and paying bills. What I am saying is that writing your vision and making it simple is a godly thing to do. Above all else, that's what a budget does. I feel that all of us need to be prepared on a moment's notice to lay our budget at the feet of Jesus Christ as a sign of our love and commitment to Him and His kingdom. We should be both grateful for the provision He has given us, and proud of how we have managed it. Even if you have an eight hundred credit score and have never missed a payment, setting up and/or maintaining a monthly budget is part of a gameplan and a vision which is an integral part of your worship of God. Whether you're rich or you're poor, budgets are an integral part of your financial life, just like your heart is to your body.

Like I've said, how you use your money definitely matters because it demonstrates where your heart is and how it's beating. Our heavenly Father expects us to have discipline with our money after we've established the vision of a budget. This is not an easy thing to undertake, but it does get easier as you go along. In *Hosea 4:6* we're told that people perish from the lack of knowledge. In a similar way, a Christian's financial life can perish if you have a lack of knowledge of your budget. It's essential to commit to a budgetary vision and the resulting commitment which accompanies it.

We learn in *Proverbs 4:23* that we should "guard our heart" because everything we do flows from it. I believe the same thing is also true of guarding your budget. Your budget is how you honor God on many levels. From our budget (in no specific order), we pay our bills, take care of our homes and children, and hopefully, give generously to our church and those who are in need. In addition, we also should save a few bucks for a rainy day. Although we learn in *Matthew 6:24* that we cannot serve both God and money, that doesn't mean money isn't important. What is important is how we view our money. Far too often, we remain emotional about the handling of our money. This is foolishness.

The reality is that money is not a storm shelter that will protect you. It cannot provide hope in an uncertain world. It *is* a way of worshipping God if you handle it well. A budget can help you accomplish all of this and more. Don't be afraid of a budget. I promise you, it's the heart of your financial life. Don't hate your heart. It's there to keep you alive. It's very much your ally, not your enemy.

➤ Perspectives

This chapter is where both believers and non-believers land on a huge piece of common ground. To begin with, some of the philosophies from my business life will inevitably leak over into what I have to say, here. I've been working steadily for the past forty-plus years and I've learned a few helpful things along the way. Anyway, for most everyone, the concept of your budget being the heart of your financial life is absolutely true. Not necessarily everyone, but <u>most</u> everyone.

For some time now, I've operated under the paradigm that you cannot improve something if you don't measure it. Collecting basic data and benchmarking it is the beginning of a continuous improvement process. Trying to improve something you're not quantifying is akin to tossing darts in the dark—you have no idea what's hitting the bull's-eye and what's missing the board completely. I'm sorry, but I don't play that game in my business life—and I don't play that game in my personal life, either. Neither should you.

Essentially, this is what I believe:

> If you're not committed to a budget, you may be blind to God's actions in actually helping your finances improve. You cannot easily recognize what you cannot see.

Running a budget tells the truth about where you are. Once you begin the budgeting process, the finish line becomes non-existent. At the same time, the pathway you're walking on evolves into a confident journey and is therefore a much better way to live your financial life. Please believe me when I tell you these things. I've lived on credit cards several times in the past, and it was absolutely horrible. I promise, I'm not steering you the wrong way with all of this. I've lived through it. You can do the same.

Whether your heart is focused on God, or whether your heart is focused on yourself and your dreams and goals, quantifying every single penny you handle is the beginning of a robust budgeting discipline. Please remember—this is not a natural inclination. You must overcome the natural tendency to avoid measuring the parameters and constraints of a budget because you're afraid of what it might tell you. Conquering the unknown is virtually impossible if you don't get your financial transactions down on paper and continuously measure them.

This next part is going to be a little tough for some of you, so please buckle up.

If you're not willing to recognize that having a budget is critical to a successful financial life at all income levels, then I think it's time to turn around and head back down to base camp. Although we've scaled the first part of this mountain together so far, what we're trying to do is totally useless if you're not willing to commit to the budgeting process. Although there are indeed some outstanding personal finances courses out there, if you don't commit to the simple measurements and boundaries involved in a budget, you're probably wasting your time on all of this. Like I've said, it's like trying to fill a bathtub with water, but you haven't put the plug in its proper place to do its job. It just won't work for very long.

Another way of putting it is that if you don't want to acknowledge that being fiscally responsible includes the writing of a basic vision of your financial life in the form of a budget, then most of the rest of what we discuss in this book will be a bunch of jibber-jabber to you. If this is how you feel, and you're unwilling to make the leap of faith into a God-honoring budget, I think you need to just go home. I really can't help you any further. I absolutely wish you the best of luck. Truly.

Think of this point in our journey up the mountain as a mini base camp along the road of scaling the heights of Mt. Budgeting. The warning sign on the pathway I'm pointing at right now tells you that it's now time to <u>really</u> commit to the important parameters of maintaining a monthly budget. I hope you'll stay with me as we continue to climb this mountain together. I actually have some interesting stories to tell you along the way. Although I've been battered a few times along my own journey, God has taught me many wonderful lessons during my own ascent. I really want you to learn these things also.

➤ My Story

In no way did I know how to budget when I was a young man. It was something God had to slowly teach me, step by step. Indeed, it didn't happen all at once. It took many years of commitment and constant adjustments and improvements. As I look back on it, the unnatural commitment to exercising my financial heart has been a marathon, not a hundred-yard dash. No matter how much money I make or I don't make, I cannot envision a time when I won't maintain a budget. Even when I was upside-down in my monthly income vs. outgoing bills (on more than one occasion), I maintained a monthly budget. Ironically, I found it to be incredibly important to know how broke I really was. It totally stinks to think that you're not broke, but you actually are. This is a formula for extreme frustration. There is literally nothing good about it.

I sense that the fear of the unknown is out there with many of you. Please believe me when I tell you that it's better to quantify a bad-news budget than to merely say, "I'm gonna have to do a budget one day." That's not good enough. <u>Today</u> is that day. It isn't hard. The vast majority of budgeting lies within the basic debits and credits of your checking account.

I'm sorry to be so blunt, but it's time to put your big boy or girl pants on.

We're fortunate today in that having viable spreadsheet software to utilize for maintaining a budget is readily available for most of us. Back when I was embarking on my early budgeting quest, I used an old computer which required a larger floppy drive to load the software in one slot, and another slot was used for loading the spreadsheet files. Yeah, I'm showing my age by telling you this. But hey, before computers, a sheet of paper with a line down the middle was often used to run a budget. The actual device you write your vision on isn't all that important (more on this in a moment). Getting the vision down on paper (or spreadsheet) is.

My commitment to our family budget every month includes looking at every single account we have online every morning to check the balances. Unfortunately, internet fraud is rampant and I'm afraid it's here to stay. My daily commitment also includes logging every single transaction on our budget spreadsheet; be it credit or debit card charges, bills paid online or by check, or deposits held aside for certain future expenses. Truth be told, I spend an average of about an hour or so every day over the course of an entire month tending to our budget. On the last day of the month, I spend a few hours preparing everything to close-out and enter the new month. These duties include moving our balance into the new month's budget, balancing our checkbook to the penny, and printing the final version of that month's budget. I maintain both a printed copy and an Excel file, which is stored in an archive and backed up to the cloud.

Yes, this is unbelievably tedious at times. Some might say it's OCD or anal-retentive. But I wouldn't have it any other way. I absolutely cannot live with chaos. It's an unwelcome visitor in my life. Chaos actually frightens me like it's a bunch of creepy clowns in one of those cheap horror movies—always circling around with the potential terror it can summon in my heart. I can actually live with chaos for a little while if I'm able to bring it into order. However, I cannot co-exist with chaos for the long-term. We just don't fit together.

Okay, enough of that. My question to you is this: Are you living with financial chaos right now? If so, it's time to take a leap of faith. It's "go" time. Let's do this.

I'm happy to say, my wife and daughter know how it all works with our budget. We all understand that we must live within its parameters. It bears noting that your budget has nothing to do with your value as a human being. It's merely an objective statement of the money entrusted to you from the Lord and what you wish to do with it. Your budget doesn't tuck you in at night or take care of you when you're ill. Your family and friends do that. In reality, your budget is just a thing or a tool, not a person. But this "tool" can make your life better if you allow it to.

Okay, so my budget isn't actually a person, but it sometimes feels like it. I'm doing my very best to make it my best friend, not my worst enemy. More on this, later.

➤ RYB, Dude!

Hebrews 11:4:

KJV ... "By faith Abel offered unto God a more excellent sacrifice than Cain, by which he obtained witness that he was righteous, God testifying of his gifts: and by it he being dead yet speaketh."

NIV ... "By faith Abel brought God a better offering than Cain did. By faith he was commended as righteous, when God spoke well of his offerings. And by faith Abel still speaks, even though he is dead."

This is a powerful verse that shows us that God expects us to offer Him our very best, not our very minimum. If your heart is geared towards obeying God with your money, you'll be successful in His eyes. On the other hand, giving God your minimum effort is something none of us would actually enjoy being the recipient of. Neither does God.

Try to be Abel, not Cain.

Start working on a budget. Do it now. If you already have one, review it to see if it's comprehensive enough. I constantly amend and improve our family budget. It never stays the same for very long.

Although we'll flesh out some basic details in an upcoming chapter, if you don't already have a budget, I'd like you to begin the process by taking a blank piece of paper and drawing a vertical line down the middle of it. Or, if you'd rather, you can draw a horizontal line in the middle of it. Ideally, you'll use a spreadsheet or some other software or app as your tool of choice.

Either way, you need to take the activity in your checking account and begin to quantify your monthly expenses. That information goes on one side. On the other side, list your incoming money from whatever source(s). Your checking account is where your money is, but your budget states what you're going to do with it. Each month, most of us have both incoming and outgoing monies. This is the beginning of the budgeting process.

Lao Tzu is quoted as saying, "The journey of a thousand miles begins with one step." That's exactly what I'm asking you to do before we continue with our ascent. You don't necessarily need to do anything with this information yet, but you do need to take that first step towards budgeting success. Go ahead, finish this chapter and then get out that piece of paper. If you prefer, you can later transfer it to a spreadsheet once you've gathered some basic data. There are even some slick online tools and apps that will do all of the calculations for you.

I suggest going back a few months to include any variable expenses you typically encounter. Please also consider seasonal expenses, like back-to-school costs and Christmas. If you're already doing something like this, then you're probably prepared to take a full-fledged personal finances course. As I've stated throughout this book, it is not my goal to reinvent the wheel by creating another course. Unless something changes, that's not my calling. However, preparing your heart for these courses is something I think will help you be successful when you commit to taking a class. This has been my approach when facilitating a Christian personal finances course at our own church.

The detailed mechanics of budgeting is a totally separate subject than the "big picture" vision of committing to a budget. It is truly the "why" you should budget, instead of the "how to" actually budget. I will continue to concentrate on the <u>heart</u> concepts of budgeting in this book. Once you've mastered the emotional and spiritual aspects of budgeting, the actual mechanics of it is all downhill sledding.

➢ **Let's Whiteboard That**

"The greatest need of our age and of every age, the greatest need of every human heart, is to know the resources and sufficiency of God."
A.B. Simpson

"Faith is taking the first step even when you don't see the whole staircase."
Martin Luther King, Jr.

5

Rock Bottom

Most of us are familiar with the concept of being at the proverbial financial rock bottom. Yup, I've been there. More than once, actually. It was like being at the bottom of a dry well and looking up at the smooth stone walls and thinking there's no way I could possibly climb out and reach the daylight ever again. It was humiliating and seemingly hopeless. Have you ever felt that way? Perhaps you feel that way right now. If so, I'd like to encourage you that when you've hit rock bottom in your financial life, you're forced to look up. That's the only direction there really is. But I'm not talking about merely looking up at the sky. I'm talking about looking up beyond the sky at Jesus Christ.

Only God can give us the hope we desperately need when we're at our lowest point and want to give up. The world cannot fill this prescription when you're at rock bottom. No other person can, either. Only God can give us hope. It belongs to Him. Hope is by Him, for Him, and through Him.

Why is Jesus our only true hope? Let me first ask you this. When Jesus was being hammered into the cross, did He give up? Thankfully, no. He had a mission to accomplish and He could see beyond His low moment. When Jesus was being tortured, whipped, beaten, and spat at, what did He do? He prayed. He endured. He walked through His suffering. And He persevered unto victory. If you ask me, that's a really good template to live by. That's just one of the many reasons why He is our only hope. Truthfully, if Jesus is the Lord of your life, you really don't have any other choice. Followers of Christ are just that—followers. He is the Way, and we must follow Him.

The nineties were brutally difficult on me. Without going into any unnecessary details, I experienced the pain of divorce and the humiliation of bankruptcy. While I certainly didn't live a life of luxury during the time leading up to those unfortunate events, most everyone today can understand just how expensive it is to live in our society. When you toss in having to start over, it's easy to fall into a financial down-spiral that lands you in a terrifying chasm of utter hopelessness. When I was at the bottom of that financial well, I had no idea how I was going to crawl out. Everything seemed bleak. It was extremely embarrassing. Prior to declaring bankruptcy in 1996, I had never missed or even been late on a payment for anything. After the bankruptcy, I tried to recover from the devastating stigma due to the public record that was nothing short of a scarlet letter on my credit report. However, I never gave up, even when I wanted to.

My point is, you can never stop trying and you should never lose hope. That was the key for me crawling out of the bottom of the well. I believe God won't often bless you if you're standing still. It's understandable to be down and out—that happens sometimes. But it's not okay to cease trying to claw your way out of despair, into success. You can never give up. This is true perseverance. Perseverance is a noble and godly skill set to develop. We all need it at one time or another.

Actually, I believe perseverance is one of the most incredible spiritual virtues one can possibly develop. Like so many other virtues, perseverance is not a natural talent—it's a learned one, just like good budgeting is. Without stealing the thunder from the next chapter, I can tell you with assurance that God is still in the miracles business.

However, for one to crawl out of the bottom of that proverbial dry well, you can't just sit still and expect someone to come rescue you.

Yes, it's true that may happen on some occasions. But we cannot just sit around and treat God as if He's some kind of spiritual sugar daddy who needs to come rescue us when we're in trouble. The truth is, many of our financial woes are often the result of our own foolish mistakes. I understand that's not always the case. But very often, it is. The good news is that when we experience tribulations in our life, God is forging perseverance in us—if we let Him. If you love Jesus Christ and are at your rock bottom right now, then look up. God knows you're there. He knows you need help. He wants to hear from you. Don't approach Him with demands. After all, He's God. Approach Him as a loving son or daughter who desperately needs help. God relishes His role in the Christian's life as a loving Father.

Yes, I certainly agree that it's not very much fun while we're still "in the weeds" and going through troubles. But we all face trials and tribulations at one time or another. The key to pushing through our troubles is that we must remember they are only momentary—at least, they are for those who love the Lord. Our troubles will pass away one day. When we're at rock bottom in just about any situation, it's easy to feel like nothing or no one can possibly help us. Being at the bottom of a dry, financial well can summon feelings of isolation, hopelessness, and a foreboding sense of fear.

Please hear me when I tell you this next thing:

In every single case where fear enters the scene, that's the enemy talking. Spreading fear is an integral part of Satan's native language of lies and deceit.

Without a doubt, the Christian worldview demonstrates that when all humans are born, we're unwillingly and often unknowingly thrust into a spiritual war between God and Satan (the enemy); between good and evil. No, God and Satan aren't equals, but they <u>are</u> enemies. When you're at rock bottom in your financial life—or are even on the way to crawling your way out of it—you must remember that no human being or evil spirit is anywhere near as powerful as God is.

No one.

It's natural that most of our focus centers on what's happening in our own life. But we must embrace the fact that the spiritual battles we fight are only a small part of the overall war God is having with Satan. We know for certain that God has conquered evil through the person of Jesus Christ, so we already have the victory. But we must also remember that this spiritual war has been raging on for a long time now, and it will end one day with evil being put away for good. Until that time, please understand that God knows your plight; He knows what ails you; He knows you intimately and that you need help. Talk to Him. *Listen* to Him.

Like I said, you can never give up. When you feel like quitting because of the financial troubles you may be having—don't. If you don't know Jesus Christ as your savior, then get on your knees and ask for forgiveness of your sins. I can't imagine going through the physical and spiritual minefield of living on earth without God living within my soul. Without Him, to face the financial (and other) battles I've fought in the past would have seemed impossible. This was true, even when I wasn't very close to Jesus. Even back then, those baby steps towards God ultimately turned into a sprint later on. Perhaps that was the whole point of my troubles—learning to forge ahead with God. Together.

By the way, I'm not wealthy by any stretch. The basic tenets you'll learn in a personal finances course are helpful to most of us in helping to build a financial fortress, even when you think it won't ever happen for you. I honestly have no idea what God has in store for my own financial future, but I do know that my family and I will honor the Lord with our finances to the best of our ability. Submitting to a budget won't necessarily take you from rags to riches, but it will bring you peace and the contentment that can only come from knowing that God is pleased with your wise use of the money He's entrusted to you.

An interesting thing I've observed over the years is that tribulations typically either bring you closer to God, or they drive you further away. The way I see it, if you're angry at God for what He hasn't done for you, you may not be talking about the same God I worship.

The God of the bible is about the One who has two distinguishing characteristics, and one important commandment (among many). God's first characteristic is His great love and mercy. Yes, God is love, to be sure. His love and mercy include His grace, which is off the chain wonderful. No, you can't "good" your way to heaven through your own good deeds, but you can absolutely "grace" your way to heaven through the person of Jesus Christ, who took the penalty for your sins. This isn't a small thing.

The other characteristic of God which many humanistic-minded people fail to acknowledge is God's hatred of sin and punishment of evil. You simply cannot write God's righteous wrath for those who hate Him out of the bible. So when someone talks about God's love without also talking about His hatred of sin, you're not speaking about the God who has been revealed in the bible. The "god" you're actually talking about is an imposter. I don't recommend him. He's a fallen angel and a total scumbag.

Joining these two interlocking characteristics of God, once again, I want to highlight the first commandment, which tells us that we cannot have any other gods before the real God. Once you fully absorb that reality, you're on the road to understanding the God of the bible. In fact, I think this is the biggest hurdle every human being faces—who is God in your world? Is it you, someone else, something else, or is it the real God?

One more thing. If you're going through a difficult time right now, or are even at rock bottom, don't buy into the notion that it's because God is punishing you for something. Yes, God sometimes punishes us because we've done something wrong. But good people also experience pain and suffering all the time. When you run through the

Ten Commandments, it's pretty easy to see how none of us are actually a "good person." That's why we need Jesus so desperately.

The apostles were intimately close with Jesus and walked with Him for three years during His earthly ministry. Most of them also died horrible deaths due to their mission of taking the gospel out to an unrepentant, evil world. While a horrible form of death is probably not the plan for most people, negative things taking place in our life absolutely happens—to all of us. Negative things happen to both good people and to bad people. To believers and non-believers alike. Why? Because this is an impermanent, fallen world, just like the bible tells us. The word of God wouldn't be the word of God if it didn't match up with what we actually see. Fortunately, it does. Unfortunately, that means tribulations will challenge our faith at times.

The bottom line is that if you truly love Jesus Christ, God's righteous wrath has been lifted off of you. This is a really big deal. On the other hand, if you haven't surrendered your life to Jesus, I beg you to consider doing so. Your eternal life very much depends on it. While it's true that any of us can end up at the bottom of a financial well (or otherwise), Jesus is there for those who love Him. He is there for those who call on His holy name.

However, Jesus won't force Himself on you or your life. In no way does real love involve coercion, but it does involve choice.

➤ My Story

Okay, so I'm a reasonably bright individual, but I'm no Einstein. I've also managed to work steadily for the past forty-plus years, so I'm not lazy either. Admittedly, although I barely passed Algebra II in my senior year of high school, that doesn't necessarily mean I'm a mathematical nitwit. I just prefer to leave the more advanced mathematical subjects with the nerds of this world. If you like trigonometry, then have at it. I won't challenge you for it.

One strange propensity I've developed over the years is that I have an uncanny memory for certain numbers. Although we've lived here in northeast Georgia since 2001, I can still recite my old Florida driver's license number from memory. I also have certain old phone numbers still etched into my memory from more than a decade ago. Sometimes I can temporarily forget a name (never a face), but numbers usually come back to me. Well, that is, once I've had my first cup or two of coffee in the morning. I'm not worth shooting before that savory first cup of java.

Anyway, I feel that for several decades now, God has been molding me into a loyal son who He wants to serve in His kingdom in a unique and special way. Without question, God wants the same type of unique child designation for all of you. Whether you believe me or not, God has a plan for every single person. However, it may not be exactly what you've ever considered before. It may be something else, completely.

For example, I honestly had no idea the Lord would have me write books one day. I like to write, but I don't love it. Becoming a successful writer was never on my bucket list, I've never pursued learning more about it, and I honestly don't care if I ever write another book again. However, writing books appears to be what God wants me to do. So I do it.

It doesn't matter if I used to think my destiny was going to be doing something else. It only matters that I've persevered through difficulties, always keeping my eyes on God and what my Father wants. In the end, God's plans belong to Him, and I have no logical basis for challenging them. I'm a mere human, just like all of you.

Actually, let's not run past that thought too quickly. Being a good son or daughter means both recognizing and listening to your Father's voice. Trying to go it alone in this world just doesn't work. The point I'm trying to make is that if you allow God to mold and shape you, things will generally go more smoothly in your life. If you want God to reveal His desire for your life, He will do so—but you must listen and you must be patient. You must also persevere.

Now that I'm looking back on my own life, I can see where He's been molding me to the point where complete strangers are now reading my books. Fortunately, most of them don't hate my guts afterwards (hopefully, you won't after reading this book). Miracles never cease. I never saw this as my destiny, but here we are. Think about that for a moment. During my darkest hours two decades ago, at the rock bottom of a financial dry well and seemingly without hope, God always knew I would write these words one day and that you'd read them. I find that incredible to believe.

In my own life, it has definitely been a miracle.

➢ RYB, Dude!

> Isaiah 64:8:
>
> KJV ... "But now, O Lord, thou art our father; we are the clay, and thou our potter: and we all are the work of thy hand."
>
> NIV ... "Yet you, Lord, are our Father. We are the clay, you are the potter; we are all the work of your hand."

God wants to mold you into the image of His son, Jesus Christ. When you're at your lowest moments, I encourage you to look up and ask God to pull you through your tribulations and show you how to honor and serve Him. Cursing God for being at rock bottom does no good whatsoever. Loving Him through your troubles is a spiritual virtue. That's the only way to go if you want to live a victorious life in Christ.

> **Actions**

Get off the couch and don't feel sorry for yourself. None of us gets through this life without a few scrapes and bruises. It's not about who has had a more difficult life. Having troubles isn't a contest. God chooses a different path for each of us.

Life is about surrendering your will to the God who made you and who has a specific plan and purpose for your life. Like I mentioned before, when God is molding you, biblically speaking, this is often called "sanctification." It's the process of God molding us into the image of Jesus Christ. Every single one of us is different and unique, and God wishes to show us who He created us to be. Please consider allowing Him to do just that in your life. God loves us enough to allow us to choose Him. The way I see it, the Lord doesn't want robots serving Him for eternity. He wants children who will be heirs of His kingdom. Theologically speaking, how all of this works is difficult for the human mind to understand. But knowing that God made you to be a unique son or daughter isn't difficult at all to comprehend it. Embrace it. It's real.

As I stated earlier, I really don't have a great love for writing. When the call came in 2009 to write a novel about spiritual warfare, I had no idea what to do. While I've always enjoyed writing, and at one time when I was in high school, I wanted to go to college to study journalism, writing is not my passion. Writing, in and of itself, doesn't bring me any joy. Sharing the good news about Jesus Christ is my passion. That is what brings me joy. Writing is merely incidental to that endeavor.

It's important to remember that sometimes God throws curveballs at us and molds us into a person who you can't even imagine right now. What do you think He might have in mind for you? For someone who doesn't relish the art and craft of writing books, this is my seventh. For now, I also have three more books on the drawing board.

If I continue to follow my Father's lead, you just may get to read something I haven't even thought of yet. So whether I've thought of a future book concept or not, one thing I do know is this—God has. The Lord's plans are of paramount importance. My plans are only important when they line up with God's plans.

Essentially, I'm saying we all must allow Jesus to show us who He designed us to be. Then—and only then—does life get good. If you're at the bottom of a financial well, then look up. Your savior is waiting for you.

➢ Let's Whiteboard That

"Tribulations cannot cease until God either sees us remade or sees that our remaking is now hopeless."
C.S. Lewis

"Survival can be summed up in three words - never give up. That's the heart of it really. Just keep trying."
Bear Grylls

"Whenever God means to make a man great, He always breaks him in pieces first"
Charles Spurgeon

6

Miracles

For this one chapter, I'm going to tell you the amazing story of some dear friends. Let's call them Charlie and Faye. There is no way I can impart to you the basic tenets of the subject of miracles better than telling you their story from a few years ago. It's the saga of their unexpected financial storm, perseverance, restoration, and the miraculous hand of God stepping into their lives and taking them from near desolation to triumphant hope.

Before I get started on their story, let me first set the table with my take on miracles. Far too often, when we hear the word "miracle," we think of magnanimous biblical things, like the parting of the Red Sea and the changing of water into wine. While those were certainly some wonderful miracles in our biblical family history, that's not the kind of miracles I'm talking about. Those miracles were what one might call "macro" miracles. They were major events recorded in biblical history to demonstrate God's greatness and supernatural power to all generations. Those macro miracles have shown us exactly what God wanted to impart to us about His character and His nature from a "big picture" perspective.

The kind of miracles I'm talking about for this chapter are what might be described as "micro" miracles. These are the ones that happen to us on a personal level. Micro miracles absolutely matter to God, and they most certainly matter to us. Please remember, there is no rule that says we cannot experience miracles at the seemingly smallest levels. To illustrate my point, I'd like to point out two things: (1) God made creation to be both vast (our universe is perhaps 156 billion light years across) and minute (think of a microscope and all of the incredibly complex details of life we cannot see with our eyes). Essentially, I believe miracles fall into this same type of diversity.

In *Luke 12:7*, Jesus Himself says that the hairs on our head are numbered. That tells me that even the minutest details in our lives matter to God. What's happening in your life right now is not news to the Lord in any way. If you don't have money to pay for a certain bill, God knows it. If you just got laid off and are worried about it, He knows it. There is nothing too big or too small for God's attention. To suggest otherwise is to depart from the God of the bible, who so clearly knows everything there is to know. Absolutely nothing escapes His attention. Yes, this is a difficult concept for a finite human mind to comprehend, but it's nonetheless true. In the end, truth is more important than opinion or perception.

Let's get back to our story. I've been friends with Charlie for most of my life. To call him a mere "friend" is a vast understatement. So back in early January, 2010, when Charlie had just been suddenly laid off from his job, my heart ached for him and Faye. Both of them had always worked so hard, but they always seemed to struggle to get ahead. Charlie and Faye both love Jesus, so I've never been worried about them for the long term. But starting on the first day of January, 2010, I found myself very concerned for their short term situation. There was definitely cause for concern.

Charlie had been laid off just before New Year's Eve in 2009. He was a dispatcher and had an office job. Faye had switched over a few years previous from working in retail to driving a bus. Although the bus-driving gig was steady, it didn't pay very much. So when Charlie lost his job, their minimal reserves quickly disappeared.

Interestingly, this is when the miracle process actually began.

When you're hit with extreme adversity, people typically attempt to either hide in a hole or take it head-on. It seems to me that the natural inclination is to just hide. But since trying to hide from your enemy almost never works, pushing through your difficulties is the only way to go. So when Charlie began his job search in a struggling economy, he and Faye both embarked on a slow push against a silent enemy which many of us battle, but one which we don't often realize and/or acknowledge. This enemy operates as a slithery, sneaky, lying serpent that's essentially an incoming mortar shell from the evil realm.

It's the fear that we will lose our home and have nowhere to live.

It's profoundly sad when we see homeless people and we all should do whatever we can to help those in need. But for most of us, this isn't in the cards. Yes, financial situations of this magnitude do happen on occasion, and it's absolutely heartbreaking when it does. But more often than not, you'll still probably have somewhere to live if extreme financial tragedy hits your life. My point is, we shouldn't worry about what might happen. Worrying is like kryptonite to our souls.

Now is a good time to remind you that we're all born with the spirit of a wild stallion when it comes to our money. As mentioned earlier, we must be brought into submission to God's will to tame it. Once again, why should we do this? Well, I'm glad you asked....

When you become a follower of Jesus Christ, among all of the incredible spiritual things that take place, what I'm about to tell you next is among the most wonderful. I often share this concept when I'm speaking to groups, because honestly, I'm preaching to myself as much as I am to others in sharing this basic biblical truth. It's nothing short of music to my ears. I'd be shocked if it wasn't music to yours, also. What I'm talking about is something I've been hinting at throughout this entire book thus far ...

It's your family status within God's kingdom.

We see in *1 Peter 2:9* that followers of Jesus Christ are referred to as a "royal priesthood." When you bring that together with being called "co-heirs" of God's kingdom along with Jesus Christ in *Romans 8:17*, you can see an incredible family status that's exciting beyond words. Far too often, we see the world in such small terms. We struggle to see that God is in charge of both the small things as well as the big things. But above it all, when you surrender your life to Jesus Christ, you become part of a royal family which has no spiritual boundaries and has no end. Everything in the universe becomes yours as a part of God's eternal kingdom.

That's not a small thing by any measure!

When Charlie and Faye began their counter-measures against the shock of losing most of their income, it wasn't the big things that made them successful. It was the small ones. For example, because the economy was so lousy and good jobs were few, Charlie was forced to take on a couple of menial part time jobs. While this was going on, Faye asked for more overtime and they pressed ahead. The future may have seemed bleak at the time, but that didn't hinder their forward march. Charlie did collect some unemployment for awhile, but that ultimately ended. Although they had to "hunker down" financially, they took baby steps forward and never gave up. I believe that because they took these seemingly small steps of faith, God was proud of them and later blessed them for it.

Charlie and Faye also utilized some other interesting techniques to help them as a Cat-5 financial hurricane passed through their home. One of those was couponing. While Charlie is what you might call a "man's man," he wasn't too proud to study the art of using coupons to get substantial bargains. Ultimately, this greatly helped them keep their pantry full. Actually, it was amazing how much couponing contributed to their eventual success. The approach to using coupons which Charlie took advantage of is something he credits my wife Elissa for helping him with. Indeed, fellowship is important. God made us to be unique parts of one body. I've found that God often speaks to us through the people around us.

Another thing they did was go to their electric company and work out a budget billing arrangement. Many electric and gas companies will set you up on a flat billing amount so you don't have the high energy bills in the summer and/or winter. This may not seem like a huge thing, but many small things in combination can turn into big things. Remaining positive, pushing ahead against the headwind of adversity, and being faithful are key elements in returning to, or attaining success.

Charlie reluctantly returned to the retail business he had been previously so successful at nine months later, in August of 2010. At that point, they started back onto the path of financial normalcy. During the time of their financial storm, they never missed a meal and they never missed a house payment. Charlie contends that, "the Holy Spirit had their back" during that difficult time. Many of you reading this now have probably gone through longer periods of tribulation, and perhaps with even more severe consequences. Fortunately, the same principles apply. Never give up and keep your eyes focused on Jesus Christ, not on your momentary troubles.

When I interviewed Charlie and Faye for this chapter, there were a few pearls of wisdom they shared. Among them was that Charlie said he realized that no matter how demoralizing it felt to be out of work, he still had his faith, his health, his wife, and his home. Instead of feeling anger towards God, he thanked Him for what they did have instead of cursing God for what they didn't have. Charlie said that the crucible they experienced helped to galvanize their family's priorities through this difficult time. So to Charlie and Faye, this negative situation only strengthened their faith in God and in each other. They both realized they cannot do anything apart from Jesus Christ. They abandoned the illusion of control.

Two years later in 2012, Charlie and Faye had a financial "after shock" while they were slowly rebuilding their financial life—their air conditioner died. When you don't have much of a savings built up and your HVAC unit in Georgia goes out, you have no choice but to replace it. Air conditioning is really not an option in the south. So just as their unit was beginning to spiral the drain, as was their periodic tradition, Faye and several other bus drivers bought some tickets in one of those mega lotteries. This is a common practice for co-workers to group together to do. You see it all the time.

Well, they didn't hit the big one, but they almost did. The bus driver group had a ticket that had all five numbers right, and was only one digit off from having the mega number correct. When the winnings were distributed, Faye had just enough to purchase a new HVAC unit. Although this isn't an endorsement for playing the lottery (I don't care for it), it is an endorsement of how God can work miracles if you're faithful and persevere. Faye's testimony is that God found an unorthodox way to hand them the money they needed to get their air fixed. It was almost like God winked at them and said, "I've got your back." Instead of being angry at Jesus for your tribulations, you should consider the big picture of what He's trying to teach you. Yeah, this certainly stinks while it's happening, but it has an absolutely wonderful after-effect later on.

So where are Charlie and Faye today? Through their perseverance and God's ongoing miracles, they're doing quite well. Faye has received three promotions since their difficulties ended and is continuing to climb the ranks. Charlie now manages his own store again and their income from January of 2010 has now more than quadrupled. Yes, I said quadrupled. In addition, Charlie's company had some major, positive ownership changes. He now has an ESOP (employee stock plan) that's worth close to six figures. This came from seemingly nowhere.

Well, to us it may have seemed like it came from nowhere. All along, God knew this was going to happen. And that's my point. None of us know the mind of the Lord. We shouldn't assume something negative is taking place when we're having momentary troubles. There are definitely things we can learn from our troubles; that is, if we're paying attention instead of moaning about how everything is going against us.

From the depths of unemployment to actually having enough money to go on vacation, Charlie and Faye have been blessed by a series of micro miracles from the very hand of God. All along, their marriage became stronger because they stuck together. Actually, they now use their home as a basis to bless other family members. Although they were financially crushed at one time, their heavenly Father led them out of a type of financial slavery in Egypt and into the Promised Land.

From my perspective, something else miraculous happened.

I've been friends with Charlie since we were both ten years old and I love him very much. Probably more than he even knows. Charlie has endured a lot of difficulties in his life, but I proudly stood in the water with him several years ago when he got baptized. It was one of the most emotional moments of my entire life. God took a proud man like Charlie and taught him how to be a good son. A co-heir. A member of a royal priesthood.

But God also did something else miraculous.

Before and during Charlie's financial storm, he always seemed to have the attitude that he would never have much in life. He was fairly nonchalant when he shared this with me one day, almost in passing. He felt like his lot in life was to only struggle. This, of course, broke my heart. While I totally detest any of that unbiblical "prosperity gospel" nonsense, I also don't believe tribulations in a Christian's life happen without there being an eternal reason or purpose for it. So watching Charlie actually have a little prosperity in his life is heartwarming to a degree I cannot adequately describe with mere words. The reason is not only my love for Charlie and Faye, but it's also because I can see my heavenly Father's presence in action.

Without a doubt, seeing God in action is more valuable than all of the money in the world. At least, to me it is.

Seeing God step into dire situations with His miraculous hand is not something we can predict, but it's something that can and does happen. We cannot enter His presence with any kind of attitude of expectation, but we can and should petition our heavenly Father to step in and help us when we're in trouble. Somehow, I think having a humble attitude is more valuable to God than most anything else. Approaching the throne of God with humility and respect is the only way to go.

> **RYB, Dude!**

Jeremiah 32:27:

KJV ... "Behold, I am the Lord, the God of all flesh: is there any thing too hard for me?"

NIV ... "I am the Lord, the God of all mankind. Is anything too hard for me?"

> **Actions**

Move forward. Score some small victories. Start or improve your budget. If you already have a budget, go and check it again. For example, are you using your budget to accrue for larger expenses? There is no solid financial plan that neglects to plan for the future. If you're unwilling to commit to the parameters of a budget, why in the world would God perform micro miracles in your financial life? Are you being so disobedient with your money that God would actually be harming you if he performed a miracle and helped you out of your financial woes? If you still have something to learn about submitting to a budget, that's exactly what God would be doing if He provided a quick solution to your financial difficulties. Yes, this is indeed ironic. But I believe it to be nonetheless true.

On the other hand, if you're willing to submit to and obey the vision of a monthly budget, I feel that God will be much more inclined to step into your financial life once you've achieved the basic obedience of stating your vision and obeying it. Simply put, God loves faith in Him and its resulting obedience in His children.

Indeed, I feel that running a budget is a lot like doing the dishes—it's not fun to do, but it's a relief to get it done. So let's get it done.

One last thing. Charlie and Faye admitted to me that although they have learned to quantify things from some of our previous budgeting discussions, they still haven't yet formalized their budget. Perhaps through the reading of this book, they will do just that. My desire is for all of you to do just the same.

It doesn't matter where you've been. It only matters where you're going.

> **Let's Whiteboard That**

"Miracles are not contrary to nature,
but only contrary to what we
know about nature."
Augustine

"Do you believe in miracles? YES!"
Al Michaels

7

The Blueprint

Okay, folks. It's finally time for some meat and potatoes. While most of this book will continue to focus on the big picture spiritual concepts within the budgeting arena, I know some of you probably want something a little more substantial to chew on. While this won't be a line-by-line description of the specific budgeting techniques I utilize, I agree that it's time to dig in just a little bit deeper.

As I see it, to do an effective job of budgeting from the Christian perspective, I feel like three basic things are necessary: (1) a blueprint, (2) a humble servant who serves as a catalyst, and (3) a gameplan. All three of these things should work together in a spiritual symbiosis to serve the fullness of executing the vision of your budget.

Let's start with the blueprint.

As we've discussed at length, the heart of your financial life is a robust, comprehensive budget. Every single penny in your financial life should flow through it. Specifically, a budget spreadsheet is an incredibly important tool because it's the detailed blueprint of your budget. If you've avoided doing a formalized spreadsheet or written budget, then it's time to put that bad habit behind you for good. Bad habits always end up stealing joy from your life. Effective new habits and practices enhance it.

You very well may be able to get by in life without having a written budget. However, I don't believe you can fully succeed in serving God if you neglect to commit to one. Now what I'm talking about here is not merely trying to attain worldly financial success. I'm primarily talking about success in your worship of Jesus Christ. In order to honor the Lord with your life, you must commit to doing things His way. To accomplish this, it's essential to have an intense focus on God's kingdom and some proper tools to help facilitate this. In my opinion, it all starts with a detailed blueprint.

Spiritually speaking, if you were to build a house on a bad foundation, it would almost certainly fail. As I continue to study the bible, I just can't see any mention of success in life apart from honoring Jesus Christ. So even if your bills are getting paid and no bill collectors are banging on your door, it's still essential for you to design a blueprint and maintain a God-honoring budget as a spiritual foundation in your life. If you love Jesus Christ, then you'll gladly show Him just how deep that love is by presenting Him with a blueprint of your budgeting life.

Now what I'm about to point out to you next is perhaps the most important concept in this entire book. I cannot necessarily claim authorship of this concept, because it's so fundamental and basic. Only a comprehensive blueprint of your financial life can properly illustrate this essential tenet. It all starts in *Habakkuk 2:2,* which tells us to write the vision and to make it simple. With that in mind, if you don't get anything else out of this book, please get this. Are you ready? Here goes:

```
God honors you by how much
money goes into your budget.
You honor God by what goes out
of it.
```

Whew! I'm glad I got that off my chest.

Seriously, though. Like I said, this isn't a new or unique concept. It's mere common sense from the Christian perspective. Perhaps you've considered this concept before and perhaps not. Either way, it's absolutely true. God plays an integral but (sometimes) seemingly invisible role in our life that's easy to forget. He gives us talents and opportunities, and combined with our own hard work, we generate income. While I don't have a lot say about what is or is not the best way for you to earn a living, I do feel that we can sometimes forget the fact that God is the driving force behind every honest business and/or money-making opportunity or endeavor that comes our way. After all, this is His world and everything that takes place in it is no surprise to God.

Now is a good time to point out that some people are called into vocations which lead them to making a substantial income. For others, their talents, personalities, and propensities don't have the same income generating potential. How much money you make has nothing at all to do with your value as a human being. It's just what our society is willing to compensate people for their particular vocation. For our purposes today, I'll just say that we owe it to both God and to our family to do our very best to generate as much incoming revenue as our abilities will allow. God gives us talents. We should not hide them or bury them in the sand.

Having said that, please keep in mind that how much money you make is a relative number as it relates to your budget. For example, someone who is a server at a restaurant will probably not make as much money in their lifetime as the CEO of a large company. However, all honest work is valuable in God's eyes, and making money is not a competition. If you're doing your very best to make a good and honest living, then I'm confident you're efforts are pleasing to God. Constantly doing your best is an honorable, spiritual attribute in so many ways. Fortunately, regardless of income level, the spiritual concepts we're discussing in this book apply to most everyone, regardless of how much money you make.

On the other hand, if you're not working hard to earn money for either your family's budget or for your own, then you may want to reevaluate your priorities in life. We see in *1 Timothy 5:8* that the one who doesn't provide for their family is considered to have denied the faith and is called "worse than an unbeliever." Did you hear that? *Worse than an unbeliever!*

This is serious business, folks. Being lackadaisical ain't gonna get it.

Time seems to accelerate the older we get. I've found that we really don't have as many days on earth as we may have once perceived. Because of this, I feel that everyone must use their time <u>effectively</u>. No matter how much it may feel natural to justify this otherwise, sitting around and serving yourself is actually a road to nowhere. If you're not already working hard to earn a living, then get off your duff and get to work. Even if you're retired, keeping busy is how God designed us to be. **Life is best lived in motion,** not sitting still.

Okay, then. Let's continue with the assumption that everyone is working hard to earn the best possible paycheck—or has already done so in their working life. If you really think about it, without both your talents and your opportunities, you wouldn't have earned anything at all. That's why I claim that God honors you with not only the circumstances which have led you to earn what you're making, but He sustains you with continued health, shields you from potential tragedies, and blesses all of the circumstances in your life from behind the scenes so you can bring home the money you make. For most of us, many hands have participated in the success of our paychecks. Stated bluntly, when you really get down to it, the money we make is not all about our own hard work—although that's obviously an important ingredient. God has actually been with you, every step of the way. He paved the way and you brought it home. It's a great partnership, indeed. Unfortunately, however, God often gets left out of the thought process when it comes to receiving gratitude and appreciation for His role in our income generating success.

Let's pause on that for a moment. Let it sink in that God has led you and protected you so that you can earn every single penny you make. Can you now see how numerous hands were involved in generating your income? Whenever I get paid, I always say a sincere prayer of thanks to the Lord almighty. I often imagine the hundreds or thousands of people who were a part of the process of generating my paycheck. Gratitude for your income is an incredibly important attribute in living your life apart from the abhorrent human propensity towards selfishness. It ain't all about us, folks. We've all had a bunch of help along the way.

Are you with me? Good.

Now, let's look at the other side of the coin. Every month, we all have expenses we must pay or we'll lose our place of residence, relinquish our car, have our smart phone cut off, etc. Every single penny we pay out of the provision God has blessed into our checking account is an opportunity to honor and worship Him by what we do with it. In a later chapter, I'll get into the fun stuff, like splurging on things and having fun with your money. There's certainly nothing wrong with enjoying God's bounty. However, we must strive for **balance** in our financial life, and in particular, in our budget.

Only when we are in balance can we find peace and make God proud. Since what I'm proposing is a kind of personal partnership between each of us and our creator, I'd like for you to consider if you've been holding up your end of the bargain. God has blessed so many of us with an income. Have you only blessed yourself with how you've spent it? If you were sitting in front of Jesus Christ right now, could you slide an honorable blueprint of your financial life in front of Him and feel proud? If not, it's time to commit to the parameters of a balanced budget. It's time to do it right now.

➤ Perspectives

The hallmark of the Christian life is filled with obedience to Jesus Christ and submission to His will. Can someone who does not love God be financially successful? Of course. Can they also run a good budget? Yes. Can an unbeliever help others through generous giving? Absolutely. It happens all the time. But that's where the similarities end. Without God, when you die, if you don't choose to go live with Him in

Heaven, then everything you've worked for on earth is essentially in vain (what you leave for your heirs, notwithstanding).

On the other hand, followers of Christ have an opportunity to honor God with not only our earthly bank account, but also with our heavenly bank account. We all know there's more to life than mere dollars and cents. But how we view money and the concept of budgeting does matter—big time. So as we continue to ascend this mountain, please remember that you not only have an earthly bank account, but a heavenly one as well. More on this later.

My point is, if there really is no God, whatever you do with your money is obviously your own business—and yours alone. God obviously doesn't play a role in this scenario. But if God truly doesn't exist, when you die, who really cares what happens? You won't be there to experience it. From a personal perspective, it's all in vain. Of course, in this case, it's certainly honorable to leave something for your children, heirs, etc. That only makes sense for everyone. But once you leave this world, you can't control things anymore.

On the other hand, if there is a God and you do believe in Him, then I don't think you want to stand in front of Him one day and have to answer for any selfishness in your spending habits. Submitting to a budget is much more of a spiritual act than a physical one. The mechanics of how to budget are important, but fairly elementary. Wanting to budget is the difficult part. Being obedient to God is sometimes difficult. But there is an incredible peace that accompanies it.

➢ My Story

From my first primitive computer (which had dual floppy drives) until now, I've experienced quite a budgetary evolution. On the last day of every month, I now print a nine-page budget file. Contained within our budget blueprint each month is a front page with totals—which acts as a type of "dashboard." It also has pages of credit card transactions (which we use like a debit card), a short-term accruals page, and a long-term accruals page. Once the file is printed, I balance all transactions, move all positive and/or non-cleared balances forward into the next month, and balance our checkbook to the penny.

One might say that the monthly budget for our family is handled similar to the month-end close for a business. Well, there's a good reason for that. It's because your family budget is a business. Without the proper accounting of the debits and credits, assets and liabilities, and verification of transactions, you could be in a world of financial hurt and not even know it. To me, that would be a type of "financial hell."

Perhaps I spend too much time on all of this. I can't say for sure that I'm right about everything I do towards maintaining our family's budget. But I do know this for sure — I've found a true and abiding sense of financial serenity. How so? It's because I now think of our budget as a blueprint and my gameplan is that of being a conduit.

A conduit?

You heard me right. A _conduit_. Performing my budgetary duties like a conduit is my gameplan. More on this in just a moment.

Before we get into the gameplan, we must acknowledge that a budget blueprint and a gameplan are not people. They are a statement and a strategy (respectively), and they contain opportunities to be responsible citizens and to honor the Lord. But they are impersonal. A budget blueprint has no emotions and no will. A gameplan cannot distinguish between good and evil. It just is. A budget is merely letters and numbers on a piece of paper or in a spreadsheet or app. It possesses no intangibles. It has no life of its own. Although your budget is an objective statement of how much money you have, and a gameplan tells it where it's supposed to go, they are not people. They are tools. Tools are there to serve people, not vice versa.

Although we have a very detailed blueprint in our family that we follow every month, my wife and I are the ones who manage it. The blueprint doesn't honor the Lord, in-and-of itself. It must also have the fullness of the human experience and a gameplan that reflects human decisions on where your money will go and what it will do. When these three things happen—and only when they happen—your budget actually comes alive.

Essentially, I'm saying that the intellectual and emotional aspects of managing a budget comes from us—the human catalyst and servant. If we're following Jesus Christ and adhering to proper biblical teachings, then obedience to your budget naturally takes place. To further illustrate this, think of a car. Having a car without a driver is pretty much worthless (modern technology, notwithstanding). So once you have the blueprint for your budget (which is your car), you must now be the "driver" of it (I know, I'm using mixed metaphors—please just deal with it). That means **you** are the person interpreting and driving your budget. This is an incredibly important function and it can only be accomplished by you—a real, flesh and blood human being. God doesn't expect our budget (by itself) to honor Him, because it's merely a statement or vision. Vision is very important, but it's not real unless it's acted upon. It's not real unless it has a <u>catalyst</u>. God expects us to honor Him <u>through</u> the fullness of our budgeting experience, not just printing a budget and leaving it as-is.

Essentially, I'm saying proper budgeting is dynamic and cannot exist in a vacuum.

Okay, so we first have a blueprint, and then a human servant who serves as a catalyst for overseeing everything. That leaves the last piece of the puzzle, which is to bring the specific gameplan, which I mentioned a moment ago. This is where being a conduit comes into play.

As I see it, in the world of budgeting, serving as a conduit means transferring money from one place to another in a spreadsheet or app. Essentially, it's a decision making process and a way to approach budgeting. This process encompasses all incoming and outgoing revenue, so this is a big responsibility. Personally speaking, through practical application and much practice, God has taught me the valuable technique of how to handle virtually any incoming amount of money.

For example, back in the fall of 2014, my brothers and I had a nice financial windfall when we discovered we had inherited some previously unknown oil and mineral rights from our mother's modest estate. It was a really unexpected situation. In the end, each of us ended up with a check for about seven thousand or so dollars. This particular event is where God really hammered home to me just how important being a conduit is.

The first thing I had to do was to pay the legal fees and accrue for the taxes for this unexpected 1099 income. Paying taxes is a requirement for being a citizen of our country and to remain in good standing. One might call this giving to Caesar what is his. After that, we gave generously to our church and I paid a few bills. We all then bought a little something for ourselves. For example, I bought a nice Kindle to watch programs and movies during business flights. As a family, we bought some brand new furniture from my friend Charlie (from the "Miracles" chapter) and thankfully replaced some really old couches and chairs. All of our plans and details were incorporated into the budget. The money came in. The money was then distributed to a dozen or so different places in our spreadsheet, and then it was done. There was no time to just sit around, admiring the money. It came in and was quickly placed into many accruals for future expenses. There was no emotional attachment to it. Admittedly, the purely human part of me is often saddened when this happens, because I really can't enjoy the money coming in. The spiritual side of me rejoices that I prohibit myself from deriving enjoyment from just looking at the money in our bank account. Basically, here is what I'm saying:

> Money shouldn't summon emotions. It's just a commodity. Putting our hope in money is one of Satan's greatest weapons against us in the ongoing spiritual war.

The one cool thing we got to do with this unexpected financial blessing was immeasurably wonderful. It was our daughter's senior year in high school in 2014-2015, so we took the week after Christmas and went to New York City on vacation. This was an incredible memory that we'll all cherish forever. And do you know what the best thing about it was? I knew God had absolutely blessed us with that opportunity to enjoy His wonderful provision.

Many years ago, we made the decision that we'll only go on vacation when God provides us with whatever funds we need for it. To attempt to go somewhere or to do something outside of God's desire is something I find very distasteful and will avoid at all costs. That trip to New York City—the first for all of us—is a family memory etched into our souls forever. Perhaps we should've saved the money for a rainy day, but we didn't this time. We went to the Big Apple and took a great big bite out of it. I have no regrets about it at all. I feel that keeping balance in life is the key to success. Sometimes, you just have to have some fun. This was one of those times for us. I know God had blessed it, so it would have actually been sinful to not have enjoyed it.

I have one last thing to share with you about being a conduit. You shouldn't be emotional about your money, but you should respect it. You shouldn't horde your money, but you should strive for balance with it. Money doesn't love you, and you shouldn't love it. Like I said, it's merely a commodity that needs to be channeled and utilized properly.

➤ RYB, Dude!

Habakkuk 2:2:

KJV ... "And the Lord answered me, and said, Write the vision, and make it plain upon tables, that he may run that readeth it."

NIV ... "Then the Lord replied: 'Write down the revelation and make it plain on tablets so that a herald may run with it."

A vision that's simple and easily understood is the best kind. A budget is a vision that serves as a basic blueprint of your financial life. When life's complications set in, I find solace in the simplest spiritual concepts. To properly understand the minutia of details involved in running a budget, it must first start with a simple vision, which is your budget template or blueprint.

➤ Actions

No one can do this but you. You must stay the course. Please don't turn around and head back down to base camp. You've gone this far, so you need to tough it out and stick with me. You need to commit to a budget. Why do I speak as if most of you don't have a budget?

Because most of you don't. At least, not in the way I am proposing. Whether you're rich or you're poor, you need a budget.

With all of my heart, I feel that you cannot honor God if you're sitting still in your financial life. You just can't. If you're sitting still, you're probably focusing too much on yourself. Let's get organized. It will bless you in ways you can't even imagine. The time is now.

You are the humble servant who needs to write the blueprint and apply the gameplan. God won't force you to do it. You need to determine that you want to do it. Getting financially organized and pushing ahead in a balanced fashion is the way to live a robust and God-honoring financial life. Don't be the one who looks back with regret about your lack of honoring God with your money. Show Him your love by your obedience.

> ## ➢ Let's Whiteboard That

"For every minute spent organizing, an hour is earned."

Benjamin Franklin

8

The Accountant

My wife Elissa absolutely loves the movie of the same name of this chapter. It stars Ben Affleck and it's a pretty interesting story about a guy who is not only a financial genius of sorts, but he's also pretty effective at shooting-up bad guys. Of course, this is a fictional accountant and a made up story, so I'm not about to suggest you do anything violent or aggressive. Well, except to perhaps use God's spiritual weapon (the bible) in warfare against Satan and his army of demons (yes, they are real). Anyway, "the accountant" in our life has actually been around for many years now, and he serves us well. I truly wish our accountant was as cool as the movie character. But alas, he is not. Actually, our accountant is a bit of a nerd. More on this in a moment.

Earlier in the book, I mentioned you should consider personifying your budget with a name and/or a gender identifier. The reason for this is because it's the beginning of an important (although an admittedly contrived) concept that's helpful in diminishing the division in your marriage which the handling money often summons. This concept also applies to those who are single, but in an obviously different way due to fact that only one person is involved. Anyway, this concept may sound a little bit silly at first, but please bear with me.

In order to carry out the instructions from the human catalyst element of running your budget, you need an actual human being who is emotionally in control and who simply tabulates the dollars and cents. At its core, basic accounting is a series of debits and credits. Like I mentioned in the last chapter, the blueprint itself is not actually a person. It's merely an accounting of transactions and a statement of reality. You and your spouse (if that applies) are the human catalysts. Blueprints are merely a series of numbers. Humans have feelings and emotions and can make decisions. Blueprints do not, and an effective accountant should not. A good accountant is rigidly objective and always tells the unvarnished truth.

Before we go any further, I have a quick question for you. Are you truly ready for the reality of a budget? Are you ready to stop hiding from what you instinctively know to be true? I've obviously been challenging you with this concept throughout this book thus far. If you're ready to bravely push ahead and put your fears and/or distaste for budgeting behind, you need to hire a mythical accountant to do the grunt work for you. This is especially important for married couples. I believe it to be of paramount importance that both spouses in a marriage view their specific budget and "the accountant" who handles it as being totally outside of your marriage. A budget does not love you. It just is. Husbands and wives love each other, not the accountant. You cannot let the reality of your budget fall onto either one of your shoulders. Moreover, you cannot create heroes and villains in your marriage. This is a recipe for absolute disaster.

Over the years, Elissa and I have slowly and unknowingly developed the mythical person who we refer to as "the accountant" in our budgetary affairs. Personifying a mythical figure who is managing our basic accounting needs has shown itself to be very effective because humans obviously are not mere machines. We have a will, an intellect, and emotions. The trap that Satan uses against couples who have not evolved in their basic handling of money is that whoever pays the bills in the family almost always ends up wearing the tag of bad guy (or girl). This, of course, is exactly what the enemy wants—dissention in a marriage. It's been said that money is the cause of a lot of divorces. That's easy to see, but equally easy to fix. How so?

Like I said, you need to hire an accountant.

No, I'm not necessarily talking about a real person. But rather, a personification. If you can afford to hire a real accountant, then more power to you. However, most of us can't afford one. In my case, I don't *want* one. The accountant we "hired" (me) does a pretty darn good job. He's had many years of practice in executing our financial plan, and he knows our finances like the back of his hand. Like I said, in our family, I am the one who fills the role of the accountant. This neither puts me in a superior position to my wife, nor her in a superior position to me. This is an important concept to utilize so you don't hate each other over money matters which will cause many problems in your marriage. Vilifying your spouse is exactly what the enemy wants.

Far more than merely performing the duty of being the accountant, I am a husband and I am a father. My accounting duties have very little to do with those godly roles and their biblical responsibilities, other than sacrificing for my family. The accountant in our family brings forth the information and we all deal with its reality. Hiring a mythical accountant and giving him/her a name accomplishes something critical towards finding budgeting peace—it pushes the reality of your lack of financial strength (or abundance) onto something that's outside of your marriage. This is important because the person in the marriage who doesn't do the basic accounting often becomes angry and frustrated at their spouse who actually does the accounting because of the lack of money to purchase certain things. For those who have an abundance of money to manage, money can and often does become a source of marital discord.

However, when you hire an "accountant" to handle the grunt work of your finances, you've essentially moved the accounting function outside of your marriage. The accountant in your life should be a personification of both you and your spouse's combined vision. When this happens, the accountant can take the heat for financial difficulties or disagreements, instead of either spouse having to do so. Like I said, vilifying your spouse is exactly what Satan wants to happen, but you can prevent this. Don't allow the bitter root of financial stress to grow up in your marriage. Divorce over matters of money is an absolute tragedy.

I honestly cannot begin to tell you how important this concept is. Creating a mythical accountant ends up doing an effective job of deflating the frustration that's almost always projected onto the person in your marriage who unwillingly becomes the villain for simply performing a necessary family accounting function. No one should be pushed into being the bad guy/gal for merely stating the cold hard facts about how much money you have … or don't have.

Like I said, it's okay to be broke and trying to fix it, but it's not okay to not know you're broke. Improving your financial situation absolutely requires change. When you employ an accountant like I'm suggesting, the reality of your situation is not only objectively stated for you (and your spouse) to see, but the simple management of your budget in this way avoids the silly good guy/bad guy scenario in your life and/or marriage. While it's true that creating a villain in your marriage is an elementary trick Satan utilizes to create dissention, it can easily be overcome with some simple steps. Unfortunately, Satan's effort to destroy your financial life and keep you in bondage is a cherished play he calls over-and-over. It's my ardent hope and desire that you'll hire an "accountant" to counter-attack this simple-but-effective gameplan against many people, especially married couples.

For those of you who are single, you obviously don't have a spouse to deal with at this time. However, the attack against you is also real. In the case of a single person, God often becomes the target of your animosity when dealing with a budget. This is obviously a slippery slope, indeed. So creating an accountant can serve you in a similar way it serves married couples. It can also prepare you for the day if/when you do get married.

I have another quick note on this. The accountant in our family is male because I'm male. However, he doesn't have a name at this time. The good news is that he works for free. Did you hear me? I said _free_! Virtually every family needs an accountant. It can be either spouse, or it can be both. The reality of creating and maintaining a budget is the first step, and using a mythical accountant is next. The actual mechanics of how you pay your bills is not really difficult—let the accountant do that based on when the bills are due. The accountant can and should actually evolve and grow in the budgeting skills you and/or your spouse acquire or learn.

Every family is different, and each spouse brings different talents and skill sets to the marriage. But both of you should be in lock-step with the commitment to your budget and respecting the fact that the accountant is only stating the facts and figures of your budget.

At this point, I'm saying you need to leave your emotions out of it.

Yes, like I said, emotions do play a role in how you manage the specific line-items in your budget. But running a proper budget should put a solid, objective boundary around your emotions and feelings and especially your frustrations. When it comes to budgeting, it doesn't matter how you feel. It only matters what is real.

➢ Perspectives

If you'll notice, the concept of a mythical accountant is a concept which can apply to both Christians and to non-Christians. To the Christian, we feel that following Jesus Christ is the only way to be forgiven for your sins and to live with God forever. But hiring a mythical accountant is a good idea for people of all belief systems. As I just stated, when it comes to money, it's critical for us to remove our emotions and see our situation for the reality it is. It's my belief that the reason we sometimes don't want to see the reality of our situation is because not having enough money to do the things we want is extremely frustrating to the humanity in our soul.

Christians are clearly called to live outside of the world. One can make a good argument that for Christians, our money is often one of the last things we want to surrender to God. Jesus actually talked about money more than just about anything else. The reason for this is that God knows His children and He knows our tendency to indulge the illusion of control through our money. The funny thing is, it's purely fallacious to think we can control our world through our wallets. Many people have tried this throughout history, but all have ultimately failed. Whatever belief system you maintain, please carefully consider the approach to "the accountant" we're discussing here. It just may become an asset in your life, instead of the liability handling money so often is.

For followers of Christ, if you love God, you'll obey Him. It's just that simple. The truth is, if you don't surrender your finances to Jesus Christ, you're essentially clinging onto a feeble railing on the Titanic. All of us will leave this place one day, so I encourage you to effectively use all of your time and resources while you're here—and use them well. There's something much better waiting for believers after this sometimes troubled life is completed. Keep this in mind if you're clutching your wallet as if the Titanic won't sink. Trust me, it will. As best as I can tell, the human mortality rate remains at a remarkably consistent one-hundred percent. Therefore, keep your hope and trust in Christ, not in your money. Your money is woefully unqualified to save you.

> ## ➤ My Story

Once in awhile, when we splurge on an unplanned purchase, I'll make a joking comment to my wife, "the accountant is going to be upset with us." Let's face it. Purchases like this are absolutely going to happen in life. But when you move the "blame" to the accountant once in awhile, it's a simple acknowledgement that life isn't rigid and a budget doesn't run you—you run it. I'm not suggesting the accountant should have emotions. Earlier I said that he/she should not. But the negative feelings that accompany varying from the plan don't need to be the "fault" of either spouse. Sometimes, it's okay to splurge and make up for it later. What you can't do is splurge all the time. In that case, it ceases being a splurge and devolves into frivolity and foolish disobedience.

Several years ago, the accountant in our family did something pretty incredible by merely performing one of his daily duties. Every day, he (me) checks our online balances in all of our banking, credit cards, and even frequent traveler accounts. All of these accounts have some kind of monetary value, and with the advent of internet crimes, one must be both cautious and vigilant. So on a Sunday morning of the Memorial Day weekend that year, the accountant noticed that our Marriott Rewards balance had been drained down to almost zero. On many family vacations, these hotel points (which do have a monetary value) have provided us with a lot of wonderful memories by allowing us to stay at nice hotel properties at no cost. Anyway, some random criminal had called in the day before, pretending to be me, and used our hotel points to make what was worth thousands of dollars of purchases for goods in one of the hotel's product redemption programs. Because the accountant was vigilant (and later set security protocols with the rewards program), the crime was immediately detected and quickly reported to Marriott. As part of the documentation to restore the points, I had to actually go to the local police station to fill out a theft report and send it to Marriott. In the end, they restored my points and we have continued to enjoy them.

The moral of the story is, although I'm not one who really likes to hassle with looking at our accounts every day, the accountant absolutely insists on it. So I do it. By being vigilant and aware, the accountant just may save your bacon one day. If I had neglected to quickly discover the theft, thousands of dollars of value would have been completely lost, simply because I would have taken my eye off the ball.

Other concepts the accountant has instituted for our family include a flat-cost budgeting for any item in a year we know will exceed one-hundred dollars. I've found that you absolutely must plan for expected expenses and accrue for them throughout the year. By failing to acknowledge an upcoming, known expense, you're allowing for up-and-down budgeting months which can be very, very frustrating. Our accountant absolutely insists that we accrue for known expenses. Chief among them is a Christmas fund.

Let's face it. You're going to buy stuff at Christmas. By not acknowledging this expense every year, you're asking for trouble. Even worse, if you don't plan for Christmas expenditures, you're likely going to charge everything during the "season of giving" in an effort to "enjoy" the holidays. Then, January rolls around and the bills come due. In this scenario, the season of joy is followed directly by the season of suffering. Trust me, it's just not worth it. Christmas is about celebrating Jesus, family, and friends. If Santa Claus can't afford to visit your house that year, then he can just take a hike. Going into debt for an expense you know you're going to have, but haven't planned for, is unwise at best.

Don't do it. It almost always summons pain.

I know some of you don't really want to hear this—and you may feel like a failure if you don't go overboard at Christmas—but you need to remember that the abundance of spending at Christmas is a human construct. If you have the money saved, then have a great time and hit the black Friday sales. If not, your life is just as good if you can't make a lot of purchases. Most of the stuff bought at Christmas will gather dust one day—probably sooner than later. It's not worth stressing over. God's definition of success is more important than the humanistic version.

Anyway, let's get back to accruing money for regular expenses. My family and I have enjoyed some wonderful vacations over the years. We've been to the Seattle area several times, the Oregon coast, Minneapolis, northern Michigan, Vermont, Boston and Cape Cod, and New York City. All of it was paid for with saved-up cash and hotel and airline rewards. Like I said, the policy within our family has been that we won't go on vacation unless we have the money saved up so that when we come home, we're not in debt for the trip. By taking our vacations this way, we've never had that crash landing that comes when you take a vacation on credit cards, and then pay tons of interest later on for it. When this happens, vacations contribute to your bondage, not your enjoyment.

In no way do I believe in a false American Dream where you can go anywhere you want and just pay for it later via payments. That's sometimes what they do in "chick flicks," and it may seem cool at the time to be so spontaneous.

This is a terrible illusion.

If God wants to bless us with a vacation, He also blesses us with the provision for it. I've been travelling for my job for many years now, and we have a nice cache of hotel and airline points. I've made it a personal policy to only use these points for our family vacations, since each point is the result of me being away from home. Although I can pretty much get on a plane and go anywhere in the world I could possibly want to, and also to stay at luxurious hotels for absolutely free, I don't do it on a mere whim. Since we don't go anywhere until we have the spending money for meals and activities plus rental car charges saved up, I have peace when we actually do go on vacation. Honestly, it's sometimes tempting to just hop on a plane and go somewhere on the spur of the moment. But I've come to love God more deeply through obedience to our budgetary boundaries, so that's not likely to happen. I desire to please Jesus Christ more than I want to become a wild stallion once again. In this personal way, I feel that we honor God with our obedience.

This may sound a little bit crazy, but I think God speaks to us through even the most minute circumstances in our lives. On rare occasions, I've planned for us to take a leisure trip, only to have some obstacle prevent it. But in the vast majority of cases, once we've decided on where to go and when, we start saving for it. Inevitably, God blesses us with what we need to go on the trip—somehow and some way.

The accountant is always pleased when we return home and have obediently stayed within our fund built up for our trip. Although the human side of me sometimes gets frustrated with the accountant and I honestly just want to punch him in the nose, I know God guides him to watch over us. All of us in our family have actually learned to appreciate him. The accountant has a thankless job, but his/her efforts are important to God. It's truly a dichotomy of desires between our natural and spiritual natures.

➢ RYB, Dude!

Luke 14:28

KJV ... "For which of you, intending to build a tower, sitteth not down first, and counteth the cost, whether he have sufficient to finish it?"

NIV ... "Suppose one of you wants to build a tower. Won't you first sit down and estimate the cost to see if you have enough money to complete it?"

➢ Actions

Like I said earlier, you can't really improve something if you're not measuring it. Maintaining a negative attitude towards budgeting is a road to nowhere and will likely prevent you from getting ahead in life. Hiring a mythical accountant is a wonderful way to empower your budget. You can certainly find success in budgeting without creating the mythical accountant, but believe me when I tell you, keeping that function outside of your marriage is the best way to avoid having Satan attack you through your finances. Fighting over money within a marriage is toxic and must be avoided. We must remember that the Evil One hates all things that are good in this world. Without a doubt, a husband and wife honoring God with their finances is a very good thing, indeed.

It has been said (and I generally agree) that marriages typically have a spender and a saver. These are two obviously different mindsets. If this is true in your case, please understand that both of you can and should evolve a little. The spender and the saver should rub off on each other to find balance. Both roles are actually very important. Using an accountant as a "referee" helps you to find balance because you're prepared to deal with life's incoming financial challenges as well as enjoying your life.

Basically, I'm saying that the accountant can help to utilize the positive aspects of both the spender and the saver. The spender will put you into bankruptcy if you're not careful, but will help ensure that you do actually have some fun in your life. The saver will help ensure the bills get paid, but can lead you to a rigid life of merely existing if you're not careful.

The accountant can be a referee and can help you be prepared to live a balanced life. Let him/her do their job.

> ## ➢ Let's Whiteboard That

> "By failing to prepare,
> you are preparing to fail."
> **Benjamin Franklin**

The Bank Above

➤ The Concept

Okay, let's take a time-out and rest for a moment. Think of this part of our journey as a moment when we're setting up our tents for the night on a flat plateau on the side of Mt. Budgeting, in a spot where we can catch our breath and enjoy a brief respite. Before we continue, we really need to sit around a nice, calm campfire and chill for a moment. We've been trudging upwards for eight chapters now, and I think we need to relax for a spell. Perhaps we should have a nice cup of Joe as we're chilling. Life isn't all about struggles, you know. Sometimes, you just need to stop and smell the proverbial roses (sorry for the cliché).

Although I've been pressing in on you for this entire book about budgeting, there's much more to your overall financial life than the mere accounting of dollars and cents. There is a spiritual element involved in our life, and it's also centered on our heart—just like our budget. In truth, our spiritual life is far more important than anything else and it cannot be neglected. Like I've said, I feel that how you view the subject of budgeting often demonstrates exactly where you are in your spiritual journey with God. It also generally shows where the true focus in your life is. Looking at all of the factors involved in what we've been discussing, there absolutely must be balance in all financial dealings in order to experience sustained success. Please be warned, however, that Satan will constantly attempt to push us out of balance. This appears to be his gameplan against us. We must recognize and constantly fight against this strategy from the enemy.

Every one of us has been given the gift of life, and God desires for us to use it for His eternal kingdom, not our own kingdom. So let's say you've decided to take my advice. Let's assume you want to corral the wild stallion in your soul and allow the dutiful and disciplined parameters of committing to a budget guide your financial life, no matter how much money you make. So now you may ask, "what's next?" In this chapter, I want to briefly talk about what you'll gain when you embrace the wisdom of budgeting and its downstream results. We need to cover this before we reach the summit. This is important.

As the seemingly intangible benefits of following God's way of handling money seeps into your soul, your financial life should begin to take on a different tone. If you end up taking—or have already taken— a personal finances class, I hope this book will help to solidify the mental and spiritual approach you must possess to truly benefit from it. There are many wonderful things you can learn in one of those courses. It is my belief that while it's certainly valuable, no financial plan or set of techniques is anywhere near as important as discovering the unspeakable peace one can enjoy by obeying and honoring God with your money. Whatever amount of money you're entrusted with, I have no doubt that the mastering of your budget can (and usually does) unleash the real person you are inside.

The overarching premise for this book is obviously that Jesus wants us to handle our provision from Him in a godly fashion. There is no question about that. For some of us, we must put the negative financial difficulties we've experienced in life behind us and never look back. Why? Because life is only truly lived from now forward, not in the rearview mirror. Looking backwards always possesses some element of pain and suffering. Looking forward contains true hope, which is vital for our lives.

The eternal ramifications of the seemingly small financial decisions we make every day are actually enormous in God's eyes. I feel that it gives the Lord a snapshot of where we are in our walk with Him—sort of like a report card from school. Budgeting and our faith may not seem to be related, but as you've heard me say many times, I believe they are. Big time.

Without question, scripture tells us we should store our treasures in heaven (our "bank above"—more on this in a moment). It also tells us our lives were bought with a price—paid for by Jesus Christ on the cross. These concepts are centered on spiritual truths which involve heavenly currency and have a surprising effect on our earthly budget and our earthly bank account. Unfortunately, our "spiritual bank" is intangible to us right now, but it's galvanized in the heart of God. The sacrifices you now make for Him will be a huge part of your relationship with Jesus Christ forever. The heavenly "deposits" you make into your "bank above" will actually never go away. You might consider thinking of the things you do for God's kingdom to be FDIC insured in heaven's bank—only they carry an exponentially larger interest rate. Your heavenly rewards for serving Jesus Christ now, are actually beyond compare later on. It's vitally important to not squander your time on earth by merely serving yourself.

Before we go any further, let me say once again, God doesn't need our money. He wants our heart. The whole thing.

When I finally came to a committed faith in Christ, it was with an open mind and an open heart. I've made many mistakes in my life, but the one thing I think I've done correctly is that I've been willing to allow God to mold me into the son He wants me to be. I promise you, there's really nothing special about me, except that I'm simply <u>available</u> to Jesus. With that seemingly simple attitude, I feel that He's using me to magnify His glory. God actually wants to do that with every single one of us. So my simple question to you is this: *are you available to God?*

During our brief stay on earth, we face a series of financial decisions that may seem inconsequential in the big scheme of things, but they really aren't. I don't know specifically how things work in the spiritual realm, because the bible only gives us broad details about it. But when we make good, solid decisions towards honoring God's kingdom—especially financially—I just know there are many angels and redeemed souls in heaven cheering us on, not to mention Jesus Christ Himself. Serving God with all of our heart is downright heroic, but it's largely seen right now from a heavenly perspective. Like I said, adding to your heavenly bank account balance is intangible from our current perspective, but it's the one that will last forever. Essentially, I'm saying that it's critically important to remember to tend to your "bank above" during your life on earth.

Actually, that's my whole point in a nutshell for this chapter.

Becoming the richest man or woman in the world does absolutely nothing to add to the balance in your bank above—unless it's used for God's eternal kingdom. Sure, it may bolster your earthly bank account (your "bank below"), but you can't take anything with you from that bank when you leave this place. Your heavenly bank account, which is always stored ahead of you until you pass from this life, is the only actual currency you'll leave this life with.

So what about leaving a legacy before we die?

That may sound good at first. But honestly, that's nothing but fodder for one's own ego. It may sound awesome to have a building, a new wing, a street, or a football field named after you, but if one doesn't have salvation through Jesus Christ, it's totally worthless in the end. In this scenario—among other horrible things—there's nothing saved up in their bank above.

As it relates to all concepts in life, one of them towers above the rest:

```
    Salvation only coming through
       Jesus Christ is the most
    important concept in the world.
    It is either one-hundred percent
     correct, or zero percent correct.
```

I'm not suggesting you ignore your bank above <u>or</u> your bank below. They are not mutually exclusive. I'm suggesting you need to bust your tail to fill *both* of your bank accounts. Being a studious budgeter helps you do just that. I believe your bank above and your bank below work together in unison—but only if you let them. Only when we're giving God our mightiest effort during our short lives here on earth are we truly living life to its fullest. Everything else is a worldly illusion that will certainly end one day.

Yes, I keep pointing that out over and over, but it's for a good reason.

At this point, I think we should acknowledge that not all of us will be able to fill our "bank below" with funding which will outlast our death. If somehow you aren't able to leave an estate or an inheritance for your heirs, you should absolutely ensure that your heavenly bank above is overflowing with the riches of a life well-lived—both serving God and serving others. You don't have to be rich to serve God's kingdom, but you do have to be faithful with whatever you have.

So how can you fill your bank above? Do you truly want to make your heavenly Father happy? Then follow His simple commands, which are to love God with all of your heart and soul, and to love your neighbor as yourself. Society will tell you to "get yours" and "you only go around once—so live it with gusto." Yeah, those expressions may make fantastic beer commercial slogans, but they don't line up with God's simple commands. Beer commercials are often funny, but they're not really real.

I have no idea what resources God has, is, or will, entrust to any of you reading these words. For that matter, I have no idea what's He's going to entrust to me or my family moving forward, either. But I do feel like He expects all of us to be faithful with whatever resources He sends our way—be it large or small. As we've discussed previously, why would God give someone more financial responsibility if they're not being faithful with what He's already given them? While it's true that none of us knows what God's specific plans for each of us are before we leave this world, I just cannot see any reason why He would further bless any of us if we're being nothing more than petulant, disobedient children with what we do have.

➤ Perspectives

If you live strictly in the world, then you probably don't see the wisdom of maintaining a heavenly bank account. If you don't believe in God, then it doesn't make any logical sense to store anything spiritually for your existence beyond this life. You must live for now, because in that worldview, "now" is all you really have. To me, this is a profoundly sad way of viewing life. If there's no life after this one, then every single moment you live is doused with the crippling fear that it can all end in a single moment and you'd enter oblivion and not even know it. Personally speaking, this would be terrifying if it was true. Before I found my faith in Christ, it <u>was</u> terrifying. Fortunately, it's not true.

Before any skeptics start jumping up and down, let me reiterate that both Christians and non-Christians are able to live good lives if they so choose. But for the Christian, our worldview demonstrates that life is primarily lived once we die and leave this sin-stained world. This chapter is intended to show the Christian that it's a cornerstone of our faith that most of our overall life is lived <u>after</u> we die. If you're a spiritual skeptic, it makes total sense to live for now. But for a true Christian, living for now makes absolutely no sense at all. If that's you (we all battle this), it's time to put that way of living your life behind you for good. If you're merely living your life for now, then how do you think God feels about His enormous offer of everlasting life being pushed off to the side in order for someone to live their life in this world as if this is all there is? From God's perspective, that's what His enemies do, not His children.

If you do believe in Jesus Christ, then you absolutely cannot ignore the magnitude and importance of your heavenly bank account. I suspect that many of you reading this book right now have done exactly that. I know I sure did for most of my life. Unfortunately, the world will teach you to focus on <u>you</u>. God wants you to focus on <u>Him</u>. You can be the best budgeter in the world, but if you don't use your abilities and opportunities in life to serve your Father's kingdom now, you're squandering an incredible opportunity to be a faithful son or daughter before you die.

Once we continue our trek up the mountain in a moment, please keep in mind that I totally agree with and embrace the fact that there's definitely more to you than how you budget. Living your life for God has the greatest fringe benefits in the universe, but you have to want to serve the Lord of your own volition. It seems to me that God won't force you to do anything against your will. Somehow, I think Christ wants us to <u>desire</u> to serve Him and build a robust bank above so He can enjoy it with each of us, forever.

With that said, I have an important question for believers who are reading this right now. It's a question I'd like you to consider as we continue our ascent in the next chapter. A great deal of what's covered in this book comes down to this one simple question:

> ```
> Are you living your life like a
>              non-believer
> when it comes to your money and
>        what you do with it?
> ```

Only you can answer this rather blunt question. In fact, I'd like you to pause for a moment and give this some sober thought. Have you embraced the entire Christian worldview that Jesus tells us about in the bible? Do you truly believe that heaven is a real place for redeemed sons and daughters? Do you understand the reality of the promise that we will all live on the new earth one day? If you don't believe any of this, I can understand why you'd place all of your hopes and dreams into this short life here on earth. But if you do believe God's promises, isn't it time to start living your life as if they were actually true?

➢ My Story

I've always been a late bloomer. So many of my fellow classmates from high school seemed to have had it all figured out when we graduated back in 1979. Unfortunately, it took me a few years and a few stumbles along the way to get on a righteous path and begin to build a career. Oftentimes, I wish I could go back and speak to that foolish young man I used to be after graduating high school. I, like most, have learned an awful lot since then. Wisdom will seep into your soul over the years if you allow it to. But going back isn't possible. I suppose this lament is true for most of us older folks, right?

Anyway, I started writing books back in 2009—thirty years after high school—as a way to cope with the grief of losing my mother the previous year. As of the time of this writing, I've just published my sixth novel. During this same time frame, I'm also now writing this book. Over the years, I've thoroughly enjoyed hearing some wonderful testimonies from individuals who have expressed that my books have helped to encourage them in their walk with Christ. To me, this is the most wonderful thing in the world and I wouldn't trade it for anything. As I see it, this is definitely adding to my "bank above" in exciting ways I possibly won't know the full extent of until I've gone on to be with the Lord, personally.

However, as it relates to the world's success of my books, let's just say that I'm currently nowhere near the New York Times bestsellers list. Admittedly, continuing to feel led to write books in a genre that might be a bit unique and perhaps a little ahead of its time has been frustrating at times over the years. Honestly, it sometimes seems like no one really gives a rip when I launch a new novel. I've had to persevere through a deep canyon of discouragement as God has led me to write book after book, yet I don't currently have a wide readership. Perhaps that will change one day and perhaps not. That's up to God, not me.

But wait, there's something else going on here.

For myself and all of you, if you're doing what God wants you to do and you're serving Him well, then I'd like you to picture the sizable spiritual deposits going into your heavenly bank account. Please picture this right now, as we sit around an imaginary campfire with a cup of coffee, finishing up our little chat. When it's my time to pass from this place, I want to walk into heaven as a rich man with a fat heavenly bank account.

You see, when we look back on our earthly lives one day, it really won't matter how much or how little God has given you stewardship over. If you're faithful to Him, He'll be delighted to show you the many deposits you've made into your bank above for the rest of eternity. If you embrace the fact that your faithfulness to God right now is of paramount importance for eternity, then our continued ascent to the summit of Mt. Budgeting will finish up very smoothly, indeed. If not, you're probably still buried in the world, which will undoubtedly end one day. Please don't forget that.

To me, it seems foolish for anyone to put their chips down on a game they cannot possibly win. The way I see it, Death is the current owner of the casino of our life and the house always wins. With that in mind, doesn't it make sense to avoid playing Death's evil games of chance? It's definitely a losing proposition to think you can defeat Death because even Jesus died. Why would any of us want to overly focus on this life when it has a one-hundred percent chance of ending? To me, this is the irony of our ongoing sanctification during our life on earth.

Let me ask you a question. Can you picture your heavenly bank account right now? If so, what exactly does it look like? If you aren't putting much into it at this phase of your life by serving the Lord, can you see fit to start making at least small deposits into your bank above by sacrificing some earthly desires? No matter what the enemy may try to tell you, it's never too late to begin making these eternal deposits.

Don't listen to the enemy. God is calling for your heart at this very moment.

➤ RYB, Dude!

Matthew 6:20

KJV ..."But lay up for yourselves treasures in heaven, where neither moth nor rust doth corrupt, and where thieves do not break through nor steal."

NIV ... "But store up for yourselves treasures in heaven, where moths and vermin do not destroy, and where thieves do not break in and steal."

➤ Actions

Please take a few moments and reflect on your overall relationship with Jesus Christ. We see in *Isaiah 7:14* a prophecy about the coming of Christ and that He would hold the title of "Immanuel," which means "God with us." This is an incredible thing God has done by Jesus coming to earth to show us the way to heaven through repentance and God's resulting forgiveness. I often think about this as I strive to sacrifice more and more of myself and our overall provision to serve the Lord. This is an ongoing process for all of us. What you've already done isn't nearly as important as what you're going to do. Like I said, it's never too late.

Since we're still sitting around the campfire, I'd like you to consider just living within your means if you're not already doing so. There are many financial sharks out there in this world, and if you take a vacation or make a large expenditure which you have to go into debt for, the debt-loving predators will attempt to eat you alive. Let's face it. It's easy to get credit these days, but hard to pay off credit card debt. Please reconsider making purchases you don't have the cash for. It just may be that God has decided to not bless you with what you want at that moment. You're not losing out on anything by being obedient. To the contrary, you're gaining everything.

While we still have our mountain climbing "pause button" on, let me just say that Jesus loves you enough to allow you the freedom to choose between His way and the world's way. He very much wants you to desire to live righteously for Him and not for yourself. Your attitude towards budgeting goes a long way in showing Him exactly where your focus in life is. Try to please your heavenly Father if you're a believer. If you're not a believer, it's also not too late. The clock is ticking, and we will all pass from this earth one day. Jesus is the only way.

> **Let's Whiteboard That**

"I would not give one moment of heaven
for all the joy and riches of the
world."
Martin Luther

10

The Bank Below

> ## The Concept

And off we go! Now that we've packed our tents and are climbing towards the summit of Mt. Budgeting once again, we need to cover another basic element of your budgeting and financial life. It's your bank account. Your "bank below" is your earthly bank account, and it's obviously an important tool in maintaining your life here on earth. Without having money and a place to store it, we generally cannot pay our bills. Now I'm sure there are probably some of you out there who don't have a bank account and you somehow get by okay. That's certainly your prerogative. But for most of us, we need a checking account in order to function in our modern society. A zombie apocalypse notwithstanding, using a mattress to store your money just doesn't fit in with our lifestyles today.

Consider this. If budgeting is to your financial life what your heart is to your physical body, then your bank account is similar to the functions of your brain. Why? Because your brain is the place where your body stores its intelligence. Your heart merely serves as its laborer. Your "bank below" really can't function optimally without its beating heart, which is your budget. On the other hand, your budget means nothing without the storehouse of intelligence in your bank account. Essentially, your budget and your bank account are inseparable, like twin strands of DNA.

It seems to me that a proper balancing between the heart and mind is what essentially makes us human. A heart without a mind doesn't know what to do. A mind without a heart isn't really alive and can't function on its own. Quite obviously, the heart and mind were very much designed to work in unison. It's a natural kind of symbiosis. In a similar way, so are your budget and your bank account. All of your money is in your bank account, but it really can't do anything unless your budget provides the grunt work or labor.

Leaning too far one way or the other with your heart and your mind creates an unhealthy imbalance. To be successful budgeters, we must maintain balance in the world of the dollars and cents we manage. Sometimes, our head must reign and logical decisions must be made. Other times, our heart must take over and lead us to use our provision from God to make important family decisions or to help our neighbor in need. What I'm driving at with all of this is that I feel that a proper focusing on your budget as the laboring force behind your bank account (brain) is what makes us responsible adults. During the process, we cannot forget the fact that we're not machines and we don't manage our budgets as if we're robots. Like I've said many times before, <u>we must have balance</u>.

As we're continuing our upwards journey together once again, now is probably a good time to say that I'm sorry to be so blunt at times. This book may or may not be what you expected. But please understand that I'm honestly not here to tip-toe around the truth. I'd rather have one person be positively affected by this book and ninety-nine others who hate my guts for telling my story, than to sell a gazillion books and have no one come to avoid some of the foolish mistakes I've made over the years. In all honestly, I'm not here to win friends. I'm here to guide you to the summit. That's what an effective guide does. Once you get to the summit, you can see for yourself just how wonderful it is. Everything that's waiting for you at the top is absolutely incredible, but you must persevere in order to get there. Your wallet and your heart must be united for peace to reign in your life.

Continuing with the subject of your "bank below," let me go ahead and tackle a common issue that some of you undoubtedly have, but you may not have realized is a problem. What I'm talking about is the balancing of your checkbook. Some of you don't do this. Yes, I know this doesn't make you a bad person or a bad money manager, but please hear me out. The monthly duty of balancing your checkbook isn't a good practice merely to catch any mistakes the bank makes. If you're doing business with a reputable bank, there shouldn't be any mistakes. No, the balancing of your checkbook is actually for your own good.

What I mean to say is that the exercise of matching your monthly budget with your monthly checking statement is good for your budgeting soul. If you merely "round up" and consider the extra few cents a month to be some kind of silly gain, you're actually failing to gain the benefit of the financial calisthenics which balancing your checkbook brings to the party. I feel that it's critically important to reconcile your checkbook with your checking statement to the penny, and then tie the balance back to your monthly budget. Doing this is like a financial workout that gives you strength and budgeting endurance. More importantly, it gives you a sense of confidence. Staying on top of our family's finances gives me a wonderful sense of satisfaction which always accompanies the conquering of chaos.

Honestly, however, I must admit something to you right now. I very much dread having to balance our checkbook every month. It's not what I'd consider to be a fun endeavor. But as "the accountant" for our family, I consider it to be my duty to ensure that I'm committed to following every single penny to its end. While I realize that a few cents here and there isn't going to break the bank or change the world, committing to balancing our family's budget and watching over it like a shepherd just might. It's not about our money. It's about our <u>attitude</u> towards our money.

As you consider this, I'd like to suggest that you also ensure that none of the things we're discussing during this journey end up becoming a bitter root that sours your attitude. On the contrary, obeying God with your budget and finances feels absolutely wonderful when you allow it to. When I manage our monthly affairs in a sacrificial way, there is no lurking guilt about over-indulging myself with a bunch of unnecessary purchases which end up meaning absolutely nothing in the history of my life. I used to do that, but no longer. Not in a long time.

➤ Perspectives

Whether you love Jesus or not, balancing your checkbook and paying attention to every single transaction is a noble thing to do. More specifically, when husbands and wives handle their monetary transactions with a positive, unified attitude, incredible cohesiveness can result. On the other hand, when you're living beyond your means, guilt undoubtedly invades your life at some point. Yeah, some of you might be saying, "Not for me—I'm living the life." My response is that over-indulging yourself for a long period of time will eventually manifest itself as the selfish villain it really is. Like I've said, I used to love to engage in frivolous spending on myself many years ago. But time, experience, and a lot of pain told a different story later on. By the time I discovered how foolish I was being as a small-time "shopaholic" back in the eighties, it finally sunk in what a dead end it really was. Unfortunately, we all know you cannot go back and rewrite your history. I suppose all I really had left to do was to write this book in the hopes it will help encourage someone.

How foolish was I back in the day? I can remember back when I was single, I would go shopping at the mall during the week to buy new, hip clothing, and I put it all on credit cards. I did this regular routine to enhance my going out and carousing on the weekend experiences. As you might expect, I ran up a bunch of credit card debt and my entire purchase history centered on me. As I reflect back on just how silly that young man was, I can see where I had absolutely zero comfort or peace in how I was living my life. Honestly, I really didn't know any better. I may have fooled myself with the notion that I was "living it up," but that was a lie. Living a life serving God and others is what's truly satisfying to the core of our being. The benefit of living life outwardly and away from self actually applies to both Christians and to non-Christians. We were designed to be in fellowship with others. Living in a vacuum and only serving our own whims never achieves its goal of satisfying our soul.

Never.

I'm happy to say that nowadays, I only live with what is contained within the confines of our bank account. I've been a slave to debt a few times in the past, and I can tell you that it's absolutely horrible. Back in the day, the bondage from living beyond the parameters of what was in my bank account ended up being an absolute penitentiary of horrendous guilt that was of my own making. It was my own foolishness that tossed me into financial prison. I was both the inmate and the jailer.

I really hope you don't do this. If you already have, it's time to change your direction in life and turn away from frivolous spending. All it does is drain your bank below and does absolutely nothing for your bank above. So what exactly is frivolous spending? Until you write and maintain a budget, it's potentially every single penny you spend. Even though paying mortgages, car payments, and the like is the right thing to do, if you're not showing God your obedience with a budget, then it's incomplete. An incomplete financial life is almost never going to be pleasing to God.

➤ My Story

Back in the summer of 2012, I had just completed freshened-up versions of my first two books. It was then time to begin the process of finishing up my longest (to date) third book titled, <u>A Walk Through Heaven & Hell</u>. "H&H" was a rare project among the writing of my other books in that it took nearly thirty-nine months to complete. I went back and forth during all of that time, working and reworking my first two books, so it took awhile to finish H&H. A big part of the reason why it took so long is that it's a theologically deep book. It's also about four hundred pages long. You should check it out if you get a chance. It's a captivating story and has some nice independent reviews.

Anyway, I made the commitment when I started writing back in 2009 that I wasn't going to take money from our family budget to publish my books. In order to honor that commitment, I had to be disciplined; and well, I honestly had to sacrifice a lot of personal indulgences. Back then, it took over two thousand dollars to purchase a publishing package from my previous self-publishing company (they have since shut the doors). Anyway, knowing I had this deep theological story in H&H to publish in the next year or so, I created a line item in our budget spreadsheet in 2012 and began to save for it. Although saving a couple of grand or more with not a lot of extra income on the horizon seemed impossible, I was obedient and wrote the vision (the line item in our budget) and kept it simple (started saving in small increments). I believe my first transaction was to add ten bucks to the fund. After that, I made regular deposits into that line item in our budget. Not surprisingly, the amount began to grow.

Admittedly, the "old school" process for saving for H&H's publication wasn't the most glamorous way to get something done. It's very much an old-fashioned concept to save for a project by sizing-up the cost, and then begin to actually save for it. But trust me, it works. Without question, I feel that it's the absolute best way to get things done in a proper manner. If you think about it, it's fairly easy to see that our society has an unhealthy obsession with immediate gratification. God's way is very much different. So what exactly is the primary benefit of this old school way of saving for large purchases?

God gets involved.

In no way do I believe in a quid-pro-quo when it comes to serving or obeying the Lord, but I do believe that God honors obedience. Every single time we now start a savings fund for something, I think of Jesus Christ sitting across the table from me. I want so much to please my Lord, and like you've already heard me say, writing a simple vision is very, very important. So in this picture in my mind's eye of sitting across the table from Jesus, I slide my budget across the table and look to see if He approves. When I started the fund for the publishing of H&H, I feel like this mental image took place by my actions.

So what happened? In about a year, I saved twenty-four hundred dollars to publish the book. Honestly, I have no idea how and where all the money came from. All I can tell you is that writing the simple vision and being obedient by steadily saving for it brought God into the picture—and He most certainly got involved. In an odd way, it almost felt like He was speaking to me through this process.

The saving for that publishing package is just a small example of the benefits of the disciplined use of your money and budget. We also did the same process for our daughter in 2015, who had recently graduated from high school.

Emily needed a car to commute to a local college. To help her accomplish this, it all started with a simple line item "fund" in the accruals section of our budget. In less than a year, we saved over forty-five hundred dollars to use as a down payment on an economical new car for her. As I recall, a couple of bonuses, a tax refund, and an intense focus on saving for the car down payment resulted in success. And in my opinion, when you move in a financial direction which pleases God, He will get directly involved and help you.

One quick note … conventional financial planning would have dictated that we purchase a used car using cash. While I agree with this approach in a general sense, we felt led to go in another direction. It was strictly a personal decision based on the circumstances.

Anyway, swimming upstream against God's will is where most of us get in trouble. It's also the cause of many (or perhaps most) of our tribulations in life. Please think about some of the ups and downs you've had with money in the past. Have you found yourself angry at God because He "didn't come through" for you on a purchase? Are you able to look back and see that when you've made purchases against God's will for your life, He sometimes allowed you to stumble in order to perhaps get your attention? Listen, we've all been a knucklehead at one time or another when it comes to doing what we want to do. I believe that a prayerful plea for God to reveal His plan for you on something you're considering is the only way to go. Treating God like a "cosmic Santa Claus" who owes you something is always a recipe for disaster. Being an obedient son or daughter of the Most High God is the only way to go—that is, if you want to experience true financial success.

➤ RYB, Dude!

Matthew 6:19

KJV ..."Lay not up for yourselves treasures upon earth, where moth and rust doth corrupt, and where thieves break through and steal"

NIV ... "Do not store up for yourselves treasures on earth, where moths and vermin destroy, and where thieves break in and steal."

Use your treasures for God's kingdom and remember that your "bank below" will disappear one day and be replaced by your eternal "bank above."

➤ Actions

Balancing your checkbook, saving for large purchases, and not living for yourself are all honorable concepts to commit to. But there's something else. Life passes by pretty quickly, so if you procrastinate and neglect to save money and build your bank below to be strong and powerful, you'll likely never end up getting started. There are lots and lots of benefits to saving. For younger folks out there, if you "wait until later," later usually doesn't show up. In fact, waiting until later for something important like saving is a humongous liar.

It never ceases to amaze me how quickly time gets away when you settle into a routine and begin to raise a family. Weeks turn into months, months turn into years, and years turn into decades. My point is that one day, your children are in Kindergarten, and the next day, they want to borrow the car to go out with their friends. Committing to saving even small amounts now—but doing it faithfully—is a roadmap to future success. It's an acknowledgement that you expect to live for awhile, and spending all of your money each month without saving anything is a dangerous practice, indeed.

In a nutshell, since time passes by very quickly, changing your minimal or non-saving habits can change the future destination of your entire financial life down the road. These small steps you take now will change your direction, inch by inch, and step by step. Essentially, I'm saying that you don't need to make tons of money to be faithful. You need to be <u>faithful</u> to be faithful.

To this day, we honestly don't save nearly as much as we should. Even as I write this book, I'm aiming this section right at myself. I think you'll find some great information on the mechanics of saving in a solid personal finances course, which I hope you'll invest in (if you already haven't). Once again, my purpose right now is to convince you of the "why" budgeting is so important. There are many others who are qualified to give you the "how to." Indeed, I'll continue to share some examples of concepts which have helped me over the years, but my goal is to simply stir your heart strings.

One last thing on this subject. If you want to invest in fancy software or apps which will help you run your budget, then do what you feel is right or what makes you the most comfortable. My approach is to utilize a simple spreadsheet and stay on top of all of the details. It's not fancy, but it does work. The actual mechanics of budgeting aren't nearly as important as your <u>desire</u> to budget. Your actual money is located in your bank account (bank below). Your budget merely interprets your checking account balance and demonstrates its stated vision.

➢ Let's Whiteboard That

"If a person gets his attitude toward money straight, it will help straighten out almost every other area in his life."
Billy Graham

Open Hand

Throughout our journey thus far, we've already discussed the importance of having an open mind (chapter 2) and an open heart (chapter 4). These are both important weigh stations on our mission, which is a successful ascent to the summit of Mt. Budgeting. To complete our trio of "open" subjects, it's now time to talk about having an open hand. Our journey simply cannot be complete without covering this topic.

What does it mean? It means <u>giving</u>. Big time giving to God and to others. It means giving to your church. It means sharing your talents <u>and</u> your wallet in an effort to advance God's kingdom. It even means giving to yourself. But most importantly, it means emulating Christ, who gave His life to save us from our sins. At its core, having an open hand means focusing outward on others, not inward on our self.

Before we go any further, let me make it clear that what I have to say in this chapter in no way involves the long-standing debate on how much a Christian should give. Some Christians believe in tithing, while others believe the Old Testament giving structure was abolished with the new covenant. Whatever you believe is between each of you and God. This journey has nothing to do with how much money you give. For that matter, it has nothing to do with how much money you make. It's about your focus in life and your faith as demonstrated by your attitude towards budgeting.

For the purposes of this chapter, our journey is centered on the common ground between both of the primary Christian giving camps, which as mentioned, are tithing and new covenant joyful giving. Of course, the common ground focus I'm speaking of is the human heart. When you examine the heart as it relates to giving, how much you actually give isn't nearly as important as how little you want to get away with giving to God (if that applies). If Jesus is Lord of your life, do you really feel the need to merely give Him a minimal amount? Further, are you only giving to God from your excess? More specifically, does your giving demonstrate how much you believe in God's promises of a joyful, eternal life? Remember, scripture tells us it's impossible to please God without faith.

My basic question to you is this ... whether you believe in a mandatory tithe, a tithe as a guideline, or just "joyful giving," are you giving God the minimum amount possible? Are you merely "tipping" God, or are you trying to advance the kingdom by including your wallet in the process? Are you trying to throw whatever money you feel obligated to give God on the table and then walking away? Or, are you reluctantly giving so you can get on with the other "more important" things in your life? If so, I think it's time to reconsider your position. There's no scenario I can see where you can think of God in such a lowly fashion and still move ahead in your faith. Having faith in Christ means embracing all that He has to say, not just the parts you like.

The subject of giving was a difficult one for me when we started back to church in 2004. It had literally been decades since I had trusted a church enough to join one. Admittedly, I used to buy into all of the lies about, "churches just want your money and nothing else," etc. That kind of thinking is purely humanistic in nature and has no place in the life of a follower of Jesus Christ. My thinking used to be centered on how much (or how little) I gave. This attitude misses the point of giving, completely.

What was missing was my <u>desire</u> to give. My desire to give was absolutely a wild stallion. Deep down, I felt like I'd be stealing from my own selfish desires and dreams by giving away money to the church and worthwhile charities. This was an incredibly foolish and selfish perspective, and I'm embarrassed to put this on paper. But it's true. If this is your current attitude, don't feel badly. We're all actually born this way. We all must overcome this self-focus and totally embrace our positions as sons/daughters of the most high God. To do less is to reject the Lord's offer of being a part of His royal priesthood and co-heirs of the kingdom.

Let's face it. None of us are getting out of this life alive (the rapture subject notwithstanding). However, we'll all live forever. If you haven't yet discovered the joyful desire to give generously to God's kingdom, then I'd like to suggest you go back to "The Bank Above" chapter. I'd also suggest you consider this—you can't just throw money at God and expect everything to be okay. In that scenario—which is not uncommon—it's like tipping a valet to serve you and then telling them to get out of your face. Although this is often the natural person's attitude towards God when we're born, it must be overcome with the truth. We must keep eternity in clear focus, not merely our current situation.

So what is the truth? The Truth is Jesus Christ. He is God among us. He will bear the scars of our sins and will wear them forever. Because of this, God deserves much more than a mere tip every month. Your entire budget, down to the last penny, should honor the King of kings. For the Christian, our actions must match our beliefs. It's not good enough to just go to church on Sunday and appear to be pious. It's also not good enough to just throw your money at God like He's there to merely serve you. The only thing that makes sense is that we follow God's commands to be good stewards of whatever money He entrusts to us. We must be obedient managers of our money and givers of God's bounty with a joyful heart. This life isn't about us. It's about Jesus and His ongoing conquest over evil.

I believe one of the reasons people tend to be so naturally conservative with giving is that the church has been woefully deficient in teaching people about the glory of heaven and our ultimate eternity on the new earth. The implications of what the bible has to say about our life after our death is both gargantuan and beautiful. With Satan so entrenched in our world, however, we're born thinking we have to do everything we can before we die or we'll miss out on the best things in life.

This is a straight-up lie.

The best things in life lie ahead in heaven with Jesus Christ and ultimately on the new earth. When we examine the glory of heaven and the enormous eternal possibilities it entails, the burden to "live it up while you can" is lifted off of our shoulders. When we have truly embraced God's promises of a pain-free eternity, it's much easier to let go of the stranglehold we have on living our life to its maximum before we die.

Have you ever considered this before? Has your desire to not miss out on anything caused you to hold back on giving to God and to others? Has your desire to live out your bucket list held you back in being a generous giver? If so, you've actually been living in a financial prison because you're trying to hold onto something that cannot last. This is an absolute dead end.

Only by keeping the glory of heaven and God's promises regarding the new earth in focus can we release our iron-grip on our wallets and use our resources for eternity, instead of for merely today.

➤ Perspectives

Yes, of course, non-Christians are also known to be generous givers. In some cases, they're even better than Christians. I totally get that. Sometimes, Christians can learn from non-Christians in this area. While I'm not interested at all in trotting out statistics to see "who gives more" (giving is not a contest), I am interested in laying out the motivation to give on the table for all of us to examine and consider.

Once again, the two commandments are to love God with all of our heart and soul, and to love our neighbor as our self. For the Christian, it starts with God. To truly love God is to also automatically love your neighbor—if you follow God's formula for life. You can love God with everything you have, but if you're neglecting to love your neighbor as yourself, you're only following fifty-percent of His commands. I'm sorry, but that's not very impressive. You must do both. Your love for the Lord is incomplete unless you're following both commands because God designed them to be inseparable.

What I have to say next will undoubtedly rub some of you the wrong way, but I think it has to be said.

At first blush, giving generously to others appears to be a transaction between fellow human beings. It is both noble and wonderful. But if you don't love God first, then what is it that you're actually accomplishing by giving to those in need? Simply this ... you're serving your fellow man or woman in a wonderful way. There are obviously many, many people in our communities who are in need. No matter what belief system you maintain, this is a very good thing, indeed. But for those who don't also love God, you're missing out on the formula that the creator of all things designed. Although I admire the actions of those who give generously to fellow human beings, if one doesn't also love God, I just can't shake the feeling that the motivation behind this type of action has more to do with making the givers feel good about themselves than it is for anything else.

Feeling good is a good thing, but pleasing God is better.

Once again, I admire generous giving to others, but the motivation must be to first please God and to follow His commands. If you fail to do this, then generous giving to others is often an action to promote one's own good feelings. Now this may sound a bit harsh, but I didn't make the rules, here. I'm merely calling the shots as I've observed them over the years. If you give to others but you don't also love God, then you're missing out on adding some wonderful deposits to your "bank above." This means you're missing out on the fullness of giving.

I'm sorry, but I just cannot see it any other way. Loving God and loving your neighbor are a package deal. You cannot separate them. Christians who love God but who don't love their neighbor are just as guilty and as far away from pleasing God as are non-Christians who love their neighbor but who don't love God.

You must do both. That's how God has ordered this world.

➤ My Story

When I was fifteen years old and living with my family outside of Philadelphia, I took on a newspaper route. It wasn't really a "job" per se, but I made a few bucks from it. When I turned sixteen a few months later, I got my first actual job. This was in 1977 during my junior year in high school. It was then that I started working part time with my awesome stepmom Peggy at a 24-hour restaurant, which was owned and operated by a Greek family. The restaurant is now gone, but it remains galvanized in my memory. It was called "El Greco." My starting wage was a whopping $2.10 per hour. I started out working midnight to eight a.m. on the weekends, which was a very difficult schedule to maintain for a student. Later on, during my one-year of employment at El Greco, I expanded to working from midnight until ten a.m., and also Tuesday afternoons after school from three to nine. It was a pretty busy schedule, for sure.

My actual job functions were brutal. I was a dishwasher and a night-time janitor. I was the guy who had the unenviable task of cleaning up the bathrooms after the drunks came in at three am and left a mess. No, this wasn't glamorous work at all. But I'll tell you what—it forged in me a work ethic which I maintain to this day. At the end of the school year, I ended up returning to Florida to graduate high school with my dearest friends; many of whom I still maintain deep friendships with. During that year of working at El Greco, I not only learned the value of honorable, hard work, I also learned how to manage and save money. By the time I moved back to Florida, I had about five hundred dollars saved. Now that may not sound like much, but when you adjust for today's dollars, and also consider the fact that this was a part-time job for a sixteen year old making a couple of bucks an hour, that was a pretty good chunk of change.

My point in all of this is that since my dishwashing days at El Greco, I've always had a particular appreciation for whoever is providing my income. I may not be the smartest guy in the room, but I'm not afraid of good, old-fashioned, hard work. Like I mentioned in an earlier chapter, I feel like God honors me with the opportunity to earn my paycheck. I absolutely must honor him with how I spend (or save) it. But that's not all. Back then, although I was a pretty good saver, I wasn't a very good giver. I had to learn how to become one as my life in Christ developed. Being a good budgeter and manager of money is valuable, but it's incomplete without generous giving also having a seat at your budgeting table.

Like I've mentioned, having the <u>heart</u> of a giver is what's so incredibly important. Now I'm not talking about giving money to make yourself feel better or to gain a tax advantage. I'm talking about giving because you want to honor your Father in heaven and to advance our kingdom. Notice I didn't say "His" kingdom or "my" kingdom. I said "our" kingdom. And that's my point. All followers of Jesus Christ have a vested stake in what goes on during our lifetime. Please consider using your resources well, including giving to God and to others. Advance the kingdom by finding the generous heart that always accompanies a surrendered life to Christ.

Although I learned the basics of how to earn, manage, and save money while I was working at El Greco, I wish my spiritual life had been as robust and complete. Sometimes, I yearn to go back in time so I can make up for the lost ground I squandered with my lack of giving as a younger man, but it's too late for that. Fortunately, God forgives past mistakes and lovingly accepts ongoing generosity.

Please consider investing in the kingdom by opening your hand—even if it's just a little bit at a time. If you already give, please consider giving more. After all, the deposits we make into our heavenly bank account are the ones which will never rot or expire. I don't know about you, but that's what I want to save for.

➤ RYB, Dude!

Ecclesiastes 5:13

KJV ... "There is a sore evil which I have seen under the sun, namely, riches kept for the owners thereof to their hurt."

NIV ... "I have seen a grievous evil under the sun: wealth hoarded to the harm of its owners."

➤ Actions

Because of how much I talk about it, I'm obviously a big believer in vision. Vision allows you to see your past, present, and future with clarity. Once again, when it comes to giving, I'd like you to picture the mental image presented in previous chapters where you're sitting across the table from Jesus. When you're deciding on how to spend your monthly income (which He blesses you with), are you putting something back on the table and sliding it over to Him? While it's true that Jesus doesn't need your money, He does love a generous giver. Giving to the kingdom makes Jesus smile. Hoarding your money merely for yourself demonstrates exactly what you think of God. Can you picture His face right now? No matter how much or how little you give, are you making your Savior smile when you slide your weekly or monthly giving across the table to Him? Do you think Jesus would be happy if you slide a mere "tip" across the table?

In addition to whatever you give, are you also hoarding your time? Are you stepping out and volunteering at church and/or local charities? Our treasure is usually led by our wallets, but it also includes our talents, abilities, and heart to serve our neighbor.

Being generous with your wallet and nothing else is falling short of what the Lord expects of us. Being generous with both our money and our time/talents is what I believe puts a smile on His face.

➤ **Let's Whiteboard That**

"God has a way of giving by the cartloads
to those who give away by shovelfuls."
Charles Spurgeon

"The time is always right to do what is right."
Martin Luther King, Jr.

12
Party Time!

Many of you probably have been waiting for this subject. I totally get that. As your loyal tour guide, I've been largely warning you thus far of the dangers along the pathway of ascending the mountain and what can happen if you don't pay attention. That's my job. Getting to where we're going hasn't been easy, but I think it's been well worth the effort.

Like we've previously discussed, there's more to life than just budgeting and how you handle your money. Sometimes we just need to cut loose, let our hair down (if you have any—I don't), and have a good ole time. Now is finally the time to talk about that.

Let's face it. Life contains a seemingly never-ending supply of challenges and discouragements. We all need to recharge our batteries to remain balanced and stabilized. Staying in balance allows us to take on life's battles with confidence and strength. Unfortunately, however, it's easy to get knocked out of kilter and either spend too much time on leisure activities, or spend too little time on them. Our enemy, Satan, wishes to push us to one extreme or the other in an attempt to keep us out of balance. When this happens, we're much more susceptible to his spiritual attacks. To illustrate, let's look at some general examples.

I know of people who tend to lean towards pushing the serious matters in life off to the side and seem to spend an over abundance of time on pursuing leisure activities. This propensity concentrates far too much focus on the pursuit of your own desires, which can be good, but only to a certain degree. It can also be dangerous to your soul if it's not balanced with both work and responsibility. Although it was a long time ago, I've been in these shoes before and I completely understand the desire to constantly have fun. It's like a type of sanctuary from the harsh reality of being an adult. However, it's spiritually dangerous if you only concentrate on this one aspect of your life. An overabundance of leisure activities will knock you off of Mt. Budgeting, for sure. Unfortunately, leisure activities often become idols in our life.

On the other hand, people like me (today's version) are creatures of duty. I absolutely cannot sit down and enjoy any leisure activities until my chores and/or responsibilities are completed. This propensity can also be unwise. In my own, personal case, I feel like I'm out of balance at times. Too much of my time is dedicated to responsibilities. Sometimes I yearn to go back to the cavalier, happy-go-lucky days of my youth, but I'd probably be miserable if I did. Because I've spent countless hours in my leisure time writing books since 2009, my sense of duty has been running in the red for almost nine years now. I feel like I need to find some balance and laugh a little bit more. I really do love to hang out with friends and have a good time, but I often don't make the time to pursue leisure activities. Unfortunately, Satan has used my innate sense of duty against me.

But I'm trying.

Wherever you are in the balancing of leisure and duty in your life, please remember that God wants us to remain balanced (yes, I keep saying that over and over). It's exhausting to work all the time, and it shows an improper focus on yourself when you don't work enough. My suggestion is to keep your eyes focused on Christ and listen to Him more. You can't just fill His ears with what you desire and expect to have a good relationship with the Lord. The world is not ordered that way. At least, it's not currently ordered that way. I feel like our lives on earth—and ultimately in heaven and on the new earth—are the fulfillment of who God actually created us to be. Well, that is, when we let God guide us. Many of the struggles we now have are borne of God molding us into the children He designed us to be. Far too often, we fight against Him on this process.

I know some of you may recoil at the idea that God is crushing your individualism, but He absolutely is not. I'm offering you this opinion from many years of experience. When I take a bird's-eye view of the many faces I've worn over the years, most all of them were absolute imposters. Only by God molding me into the son He designed me to be have I found true peace in my life. There are many things I would personally love to do (like move to Seattle, take a train ride across Canada, and spend a summer on the Maine coast), but I may not get to do these things before I die. Remember, your bucket list never ends when you love Jesus Christ. Sipping coffee in Pike Place Market every morning is my personal dream, but it might not actually happen until later on. That's up to God and I'm okay with that. Actually, I <u>love</u> that.

And that's my point to all of you.

Yes, it's absolutely wonderful to live it up and to have a good time sometimes. But if you're only doing that, you're probably out of balance and could likely use a spiritual tune up.

Okay, with all of that said, let's talk about cutting loose and having some fun. One of the most wonderful benefits of balanced budgeting is that when you do use your resources to enjoy God's bounty, you've absolutely earned it. There's nothing like the satisfaction of going on a vacation you've earned by working hard and by saving for it. So whatever you love in life, from season tickets to sporting events, concerts, trips, camping, or even doing some enhancements to your home, when God blesses it, it's all the more sweet. There's nothing like enjoying God's provision.

There's a silent enemy out there who attempts to rob us of our joy and steal the happiness God wants us to have. It's an imposter who pretends to be a friend, but is actually a huge enemy. Enjoying our life and experiencing whatever time the Lord gives us on earth to the fullest is a wonderful thing. But there's an enemy who uses a bitterly evil tactic against both Christians and non-Christians. This tactic is a liar to all people.

This enemy is binge shopping.

Binge or unnecessary shopping is a "drug" that must be avoided at all costs. I'm embarrassed to say that I'm a reformed binge shopper (at least, on a small scale). I can't believe what a nitwit I was for falling into that worldly trap many years ago. I suppose I just didn't know any better at the time.

Listen, there's nothing that resides in the world of being a responsible adult that allows for one to shower yourself with myriad unnecessary things in a vain attempt to fill some desperate hole in your soul. Neither Christian, nor naturalist, nor any other religious affiliation is likely to endorse this horrible practice. It is selfish and narcissistic.

The soul of a Christian is centered on Jesus Christ. As a reformed binge-shopper, I can assure you with absolute certainty that the hunger one tries to satisfy by hitting the mall and charging your way from one end to the other is a dangerous, anti-spiritual narcotic. Unfortunately, just like drug use, excessive shopping always has a miserable crash landing.

By the way, I'm also talking to those who today click their way towards a false happiness by overzealous online shopping. E-commerce is in no way, a lesser weapon against you than a mall or a shopping center. In fact, it may actually be worse due to how easy it is to have things delivered right to your doorstep. Just a few clicks and your spiritual drug is on its way.

It makes no sense to go into debt for things that don't really matter in life. Being in debt is like slavery. It totally stinks. Being owned by a bunch of possessions that you really don't need or want is a terrible situation and ultimately leads to depression, in some cases. If this is you, don't feel bad. Just own it. Satan uses this strategy against people all the time. You're not alone. Binge shopping, or shopping for boredom, is something that makes Satan smile, but makes God shake His head in disappointment. I don't know about you, but that's not something I want to happen.

Please remember, enjoying the sweat of our brow is a wonderful thing. This is something God endorses. However, it's not a free ticket to over indulge.

➢ My Story

My family and I have been blessed to have taken some wonderful vacations over the years. It seems that when we decide upon a destination and start saving for it, God always seems to let us know that it's His will for us to go by providing a way. Prior to God showing me how to partner with Him on whether He wanted us to go on a particular vacation or not, I never felt the peace that comes with knowing the Lord has anointed something to happen. Previously, when I would make purchases or go on trips against His will and by going into debt, I never felt comfortable. But since then, I feel the full experience of God's bounty when I know He wants us to go somewhere or to purchase something. Once again, God is big enough to be intimately involved with every single penny in our budgets. If you don't think God is that big, you're worshipping the wrong god. The real God is very much that big. Perhaps even bigger.

In a previous chapter, I mentioned that we have some rewards points built up which help us to take family vacations. They are a true blessing and an actual asset which the accountant protects. When I signed on to be your tour guide, I promised to be transparent, so here is some more of that. I touched on earlier what I'm about to say, but saved the whole story for this chapter. Here it is. It takes an enormous amount of self discipline to not use our rewards points whenever the stresses of working and everyday life weigh in on me. In the past few decades, I've taken about nine leisure trips to Seattle. I absolutely fell in love with western Washington after making my first trip there in 1991 (actually, that was for both business and pleasure). Interestingly, that's also when I experienced my first cup of Starbucks coffee. But alas, that's a story for another day....

Anyway, when the normal stresses of my career in the trucking and logistics business weigh-in, sometimes I just want to hop on a plane to Seattle and spend a few days on the waterfront, lollygagging around Pike Place Market, drinking coffee, and enjoying the cool weather. I guess you might say that Seattle is my happy place. But as of this writing, I haven't been there in over five years.

Although I do hope to return there soon for a visit, I have to show constant restraint and wait until the time is right. It's easy to say, "You only go around once, so go for it. Make yourself happy." However, that's only a half-truth. Like I've pointed out many times, the whole truth for the Christian is that we will live most of our existence beyond this life. So while it's true that we only go around once on the existing earth, we will live forever in heaven and later on the new earth.

Remember, I said forever. That's a really long time.

So many of us live our lives on what I've heard described as a type of "pleasure quest." This is the natural, default way of living. As a follower of Christ, we must balance our life with living on a "service quest," which means we're serving God and enjoying the benefits of it before we leave this place. Not to belabor the point, but I plead with you to consider just how much of a lie it is that you have to do everything you want to do before you die. Your real life living with Christ will happen after you leave this place. Remember, the enemy only needs to knock you just a little bit off balance. When he does this, it changes your entire trajectory in life. For example, if you start over-indulging just a little bit, that turns into a much larger issue many years down the road. This type of sneaky tactic is a cherished ploy in the spiritual war between good and evil.

➤ RYB, Dude!

Ecclesiastes 3:13

KJV ... "And also that every man should eat and drink, and enjoy the good of all his labour, it is the gift of God."

NIV ... "That each of them may eat and drink, and find satisfaction in all their toil—this is the gift of God."

➤ Actions

By all means, have some fun with your resources. However, please also realize that some of the best fun you can possibly have doesn't involve spending lots of money. When I shopped compulsively when I was younger, it was only a silly attempt to fill a hole in my soul that a new shirt or pair of pants couldn't possibly fill. Fortunately, as I've grown older, I've found a lot of joy in some of the simpler things in life.

For example, some friends and I have been in a fantasy football league since 1984. We officially kicked off our first full season the next year in 1985, and have been gathering for an annual draft and enjoying the league ever since. Every Labor Day weekend, we gather like it's a family reunion and spread out our draft picks over a long weekend. We cook meals, hang out, sit around chatting, and give each other grief over our team's performances over the years. In general, we have a relaxed, wonderful time. I wouldn't trade these annual draft gatherings for anything in the world.

One quick note … we don't gamble and we never have. There is no "winning pot" to collect at the end of the year. The only cost is the nominal fee we each pay for the online service to manage our league's data. I just can't tell you how grateful I am that God has blessed our group of friends with such an incredible activity that bonds our friendships, yet costs almost nothing. The "Budgeg Football League" ("budgeg" is an off-shoot of the word "buddy") is one of the oldest, continually-running fantasy football leagues in the country. It is noble, funny, silly, competitive, historical, and binds friendships that go back over four decades. To me, it's worth a gazillion dollars. But fortunately, it's virtually free.

The "BFL" is absolutely a blessing from God. There's no doubt about it.

I'm telling you about the BFL because I want you to consider the concept that you don't have to purchase first class tickets to fly around the world to enjoy God's bounty. Sometimes, it's sitting right there in your own backyard. For a few, it's awesome if you have a private plane and the money to go anywhere you want. But for most of us, that isn't something that's going to happen during our lifetime here on this version of the earth (perhaps it will on the new earth).

My point is, according to *Acts 17:26*, God indicates that He has appointed a time in history for every single one of us. As much as I detest the so-called "prosperity gospel" (generally, this means God will give you more if you give him more money), I also reject the "non-prosperity" gospel. In my mind, the non-prosperity gospel is a false notion that you're supposed to only struggle in life and will never enjoy God's bounty during your life here on earth. As far as I'm concerned, how much or how little you have during your lifetime is between you and God. We should be praying for Him to reveal His plan for our life, not merely tell Him how much or how little we expect of Him.

Praying for God's revelation in your life is more important than trying to predict how much stuff He wants you to have. I suggest spending your time petitioning Him to reveal His will for you, not cursing Him for not meeting your expectations. Whatever you have, God designed it that way. Oftentimes, we have financial troubles due to our own mistakes and bad decisions. When this happens, we must remember that God is God and we are not. Although this may sound a bit simplistic, we all need a regular refresher on this concept as we push ahead in our spiritual life. The throne belongs to Jesus Christ, not any one of us. However, being a son or daughter in His kingdom does have some incredible benefits. So go ahead and enjoy them!

Whatever you have or whatever you do, do it to the glory of God. If you have money and/or rewards points, etc., to splurge on something, do it while you bask in the glory of God's incredible provision and bounty. Enjoy what He has given you, don't curse Him for what He hasn't.

> ## Let's Whiteboard That

"We could never learn to be brave
and patient,
if there were only joy in the
world."
Helen Keller

"As long as a man is alive and
out of hell,
he cannot have any cause to
complain."
Charles Spurgeon

13

Dreams & Goals

Don't give up now. You're almost there!

For this chapter, it's time to talk about future thinking and future planning. But before we get started on the subject of your cherished dreams and establishing goals, let me paint you a quick picture.

Because of our sin nature, we're all born with enmity between our heart and our money. I suppose you could say, our heart and our wallet are officially released into a ruthless cold war when we're old enough to understand what money actually is. Take a look at the front cover of this book again and you can see the visual depiction of this separation. While there isn't typically any kind of direct warfare between them, your heart and your money often begin their relationship by hating each other's guts. In order for true peace to reign in your life, they must be brought into an inseparable alliance. Their cold war simply must end. As long as your heart and your wallet are at odds with each other, the stress from this separation will very likely dominate your life with unnecessary and potentially debilitating stress.

I've come to believe that uniting your heart and your money is vitally important for accomplishing almost every goal you can possibly have in your financial life. You can get a PhD in financial planning, but if your heart and your wallet remain at odds, nothing will be successful for the long-term. And by "long term," I mean forever. Let's not forget that all of the money you gather on earth without honoring God is merely temporary because it doesn't add to your bank above. As I mentioned previously, true wealth includes filling both your bank above and your bank below. Actually, when you faithfully use your bank below through proper budgeting, you <u>automatically</u> fill your bank above. Think about that for a moment. When you submit to a budget and run it faithfully, you get a type of "double deposit" in both your earthly and heavenly bank accounts. But when you aren't faithful with the money God has entrusted to you, it's actually a double negative. In that case, Satan gets the victory.

That's not good at all. I hate that dude.

The bottom line is this. The importance of proper budgeting cannot be overstated. Running a God-honoring budget may not have seemed all that important before, but I hope by climbing this mountain with me, you've perhaps had a change of heart ... or are at least thinking about it. Please remember, understanding the "how to" aspect of building your personal finances platform is very important. But in my opinion, embracing the "why" you should build it is even <u>more</u> important. It sets the table for virtually everything else. It's like the fuel in your tank. It is absolutely vital.

Yes, what I'm saying now are things which have largely been presented in previous chapters, several times over. However, I wanted to remind you of them before we get into the future planning stuff. The simplicity of basic budgeting fundamentals are, by no means, complicated. Believe me, if budgeting was complicated, I wouldn't be writing these words to you now. In no way would I have anything to add to the discussion.

As it relates to our dreams and goals, let me be clear that I understand how important these concepts are for most of us. I'm a fellow human being so I get all of that. For some of us, living on a white sand beach is our perfect vision of living the good life. For others (like me), living in the mountains is the ultimate goal. Whatever your dreams are, there's a good chance they'll be with you forever. God created each of us to be unique individuals, and He knows our hearts and our desires. The key for finding peace and happiness is to seek out the Lord's plan for your future. I can assure you, there are no coincidences in God's world. You exist for a purpose, even if you don't believe it right now. Very often, what may seem like a "mundane life" is actually an exceptional one—at least it is from God's perspective.

So tell me, something. Have you discovered God's will for your life? If not, keep moving forward and pursue Him. Also, I think you need to increase your listening. Listen to His voice. If you're not hearing God, is it because you're not listening? I know it was that way with me for a long time. I couldn't hear God's voice because I was too busy filling His ears with all of the things I wanted in life.

You may not realize this, but your future goals actually have something in common with the spiritual concept of hope. In both cases, they're forward-leaning subjects. I know very few people who don't have dreams and goals, and even fewer who can exist without the blessed virtue of hope (actually, that number is zero). Why? Because hope is the invisible ingredient in our lives that has an enormous impact on virtually everything we do. When I was at my financial rock bottom a couple of decades ago, only the lifeline of hope pulled me out of it without me going completely nuts. Only by knowing things would get better was I able to forge ahead. Hope is blessed. Hope belongs to Jesus Christ. Hope pulled me out of the bottom of the well. God's hope will also do the same thing for you—wherever you are in life.

Before we go any further, I have a quick caveat about the subject of hope. Unfortunately, hope can be sneaky and wear a mask which hides something absolutely hideous underneath—which is basically a type of false hope. Unfortunately, false hope sometimes masquerades as the real deal. We must be careful in what or in whom we place our hope. A good example would be a wealthy person. If you're wealthy and you've placed your hope in your money, then you've partnered with a liar. Anything or anyone outside of Christ cannot be a repository of true hope. Please always keep this in mind. Placing false hope in flimsy things like money can be a treacherous mistress, indeed.

In order for hope to work properly, the ingredient on our side of the equation is perseverance. God is the One who provides hope, but we must respond to it with our perseverance. Life on the earth right now is stained with many struggles, but hope gives us the energy to not give up. Our biggest dreams and goals are food for our soul—but only if they're imbued with the hope that can only come from our creator. So as you look forward to a hopefully bright financial future, please remember that you cannot achieve your goals without the Lord not only blessing them, but He also must walk beside you as you pursue these goals. Even when you've found a comfortable level of success, God must be with you or it will not last forever.

The greatest successes I've had in life have always included Jesus Christ. In fact, I can't even call something a success without Him. Even when I've had to do things which didn't seem orthodox at the time, I've learned to follow God's lead. Remember now, you're reading the words of someone who doesn't really enjoy the art and craft of writing. I do it because I know my heavenly Father wants me to do it, and nothing more. If you're wrestling with God right now about what direction you're going in life, please consider dropping your fight and allow Him to show you who the person He actually designed you to be is. Trust me, God's resolve is greater than yours. While I suggest you don't give up pushing forward in pursuing your dreams and goals, I do suggest you give up doing things strictly your own way. God has a say-so in your life. After all, He's God.

One more thing. The evil forces in this world will do everything they can to minimize our ability to serve God. They hate it when Jesus gets the victory and each of us allows Him to be a part of our biggest dreams and goals. The spiritual war we are all born into is real. To a skeptical mind, it's easy to write-off someone who believes in spiritual powers in this world beyond what we can see with our eyes. But like I've said, truth outweighs opinion. And the truth is, the demonic world will try to destroy you and keep you away from God. Walk with Christ and He'll protect and reward you. Walk not with Christ, and although he may, He really has no reason to protect or reward you.

➤ Perspectives

If you want to fully realize any dream or achieve any goal, you need to partner with the One who can actually help you get there. You need to be an obedient son our daughter and walk together with God, not against Him. Trying to swim upstream against the creator of all things is an exercise in futility and downright silly. To illustrate my point, let's take the biblical case of Solomon.

To the world, Solomon had it all. He had hundreds of wives and concubines, a tremendous amount of wisdom from God, and more money than he could possibly know what to do with. He was the king of a nation and he experienced things most people today absolutely long for—sex, money, and plenty of smarts. He had virtually anything he ever wanted. To the world, Solomon was probably the all-time best example of "the ultimate dude." His father David was a wildly successful king, and his ability to make an impact for God was beyond compare. However, through all of Solomon's "success," something was wrong. Something was missing. Actually, some-<u>one</u> was missing.

God was.

Since I began my biblical studies, I've always believed that the Lord used the life of Solomon to demonstrate to future generations the vast difference between the world's pursuits or goals and God's goals. To me, Solomon's story is the ultimate contrast between how the world wants to live and how God wants us to live. From the world's perspective, it's not hard to imagine most people wanting to have that many spouses at their disposal, tons of power, a huge and extravagant home, and the ability to look around the room and be the unquestionably smartest person in it. Then there's the cash. Yup, that's it. Wouldn't it be nice to have as much cash we could possibly need? Interestingly, all of these things seem to be the goal of so many celebrities today. But what were Solomon and so many celebrities today really striving for?

Their own glory. That's what.

Does Solomon's story sound pretty cool? Well, at this point, it kind of does. However, if you want to see the moral of the story, go and read the book of Ecclesiastes. It was written near the end of Solomon's life. The book is full of wisdom, but it's desperately somber and it drips of regret. You see, Solomon finally figured out that worldly success and all of its trappings are an enormous illusion, which of course, are always marketed by the devil. The first part of Solomon's life was filled with his every desire. But he ultimately ended up blowing his chance to be a true, godly man on earth because of his hedonistic, self focus.

For my fellow sports fans, we all know that a baseball game is nine innings long. What happens in the first couple of innings may be wonderful, but you must finish the entire game for it to end up being a "win." In sports terms, it seems to me that Solomon dominated the game for the first seven or eight innings, but fell apart in the final inning. Why? Because He left God out of the gameplan. Solomon's life was incomplete because he had everything in the world except what he really needed—God's involvement. Or in baseball terms, Solomon didn't have God as his closer.

As strange as this may sound, I think God actually cursed Solomon with his every dream and goal. In other words, God cursed Solomon with affluence. The book of Ecclesiastes demonstrates a very somber rich dude who knew everything was futile and meaningless without God being glorified. This is a lesson for all of us to take note of. The pursuit of goals outside of the Lord is futile at best and destructive at worst.

Some of you may be on the same track as Solomon. I truly hope not, but if there's any chance you're pursuing the world, I beg you to go read the book of Ecclesiastes. There, you'll see a man who found the truth that you cannot ignore the Lord as you pursue your goals in life. It just doesn't work in the end.

In other words, dreams and goals are totally dysfunctional without God.

➢ My Story

It seems to me that no matter how many wonderful goals you have in life, if you're a slave to debt, you'll very likely never realize your greatest dreams here on earth. God doesn't want us to live in debt because He knows Satan will persecute us if we've willingly given away our freedom in order to have some stuff we probably don't need. Debt puts us in bondage and is an absolute dream killer—especially if it's self-induced. Being in bondage diminishes our ability to make an impact in this life and stands in our way of loving God and loving our neighbor like we should. Sometimes we fall into debt for unfortunate things like medical expenses. This cannot be avoided in some cases. But self-imposed debt due to self-focus is as destructive a force as anything in this world.

Honestly, I've only found peace and joy in my life since I turned away from the drug of self-focus in my youthful, cavalier spending and budgeting habits. At this point in my life, it's not an option to not tell you the truth. So here are a few things I feel you must do in order to fulfill your dreams and goals:

➢ You must **plan**. Sometimes, pennies seem to fall from heaven and help us to get things done when we stay within God's will (see the "Miracles" chapter). But more often than not, you have to save for the things you want. Don't be afraid to start this process. Go ahead and drop five dollars into a spreadsheet line item with the goal of saving for something you want. No, this isn't a glitzy way to get things done, but it's noble and it pleases the Lord because you're involving Him in your dreams and goals. I believe God really loves that.

➢ You must become a budgetary **conservationist**. Search for bargains and find ways to conserve money. It's not impressive one single bit if you waste any of the precious resources God gives to you. Don't think you're too good to use coupons or find sales. The moment you think you're better than your neighbor because you have more money than them, pride has overtaken you. This obviously isn't good. None of us are too good or too wealthy to become proper stewards of what God provides us with. The meek (in spirit) shall inherit the earth. That means humility is a virtue we all must strive for. Pride and arrogance are humility's antithesis.

➤ You need to forget about our society's **negative connotations** with running and living within the parameters of a budget. So many of us are peer or family pressured into doing things we cannot afford. For example, if you haven't saved enough money for Christmas gifts throughout the year, then find a way to give gifts that don't cost a lot of money. It's absolutely insane to go into debt for reasons that only conform to society's norms or expectations for things like the holidays. Absolutely no one should be embarrassed if you don't have a lot of money to give expensive gifts. Absolutely everyone should be embarrassed if you go into debt to ensure no one thinks you're a deadbeat for not giving lots of gifts that will likely gather dust at some point. Honestly, who cares what the world thinks? Let me ask you this. Are you following the example of Jesus Christ, or are you lined up with and pursuing Solomon's path? Not everyone will be rich in this world. But through Jesus Christ, we will all be "rich" with our Lord forever. "Rich" in His presence, that is.

➤ RYB, Dude!

Proverbs 16:3

KJV ... "Commit thy works unto the Lord,
and thy thoughts shall be established."

NIV ... "Commit to the Lord whatever you
do, and he will establish your plans."

➤ Actions

I think it's very important to incorporate your dreams and goals into your monthly budget blueprint. In our family, we have this covered in the last two pages in our budget spreadsheet, which are the short term and long term accruals pages.

An accrual is simply a savings device in which you take some money over time and hold it for an anticipated expenditure or expense. Typically, accruals are in place for periodic deposits that build up to a certain amount. An example would be what we've talked about a couple of times already—a Christmas fund. The best way to build a Christmas fund is to figure out in early January what you'll need to spend later that year, divide that amount by twelve, and start putting the money away. The same thing applies to most other expenditures. Creating savings funds or accruals shows vision and takes perseverance to accomplish.

145

Like I've said, these are godly attributes. I didn't like dealing with accruals and funds at first, but I've grown to love them.

Perhaps this may sound a bit simplistic to some of you, and you're probably right. However, like I've said many times before, budgeting is not about complication. It's about execution. In my opinion:

> A good budgeter who doesn't have a lot of money is wealthier than a bad budgeter who has lots of money and doesn't know where it goes.

A good budgeter knows how to live with restraint. A bad budgeter never has enough money. A good budgeter finds peace. A bad budgeter is always worried about how much money they have. If you want to achieve your goals and live your wildest dreams, make sure to involve God and accrue money in a disciplined fashion. That is what true success looks like.

➢ Let's Whiteboard That

> "Continuous effort—not strength nor intelligence—is the key to unlocking our potential."
> **Winston Churchill**

14
The Summit

> **The Concept**

Congratulations. We've just pierced the cloud cover at the top of the mountain and have arrived at the summit. If you've been absorbing all of these wonderful budgeting concepts during our ascent, then your heart and your money are now indelibly connected. This is not a small thing—it's huge. It's enormous! It's time to celebrate.

But before we begin our celebration and begin to wrap things up, now is a good time for a bit of an admission on my part. During our journey, I've consistently advised you of the importance of persevering to the summit. Since you've now arrived, I want to admit to you that Jesus Christ has always been here, waiting to help you celebrate your arrival. You see, the climbing of Mt. Budgeting is obviously a spiritual endeavor, not a physical one. Once you've made it to the top, I'm confident that God is pleased with your effort to arrive here. The mere fact that God has been molding me over the years to present all of this to you, and the fact that you're now reading these words right now are of no surprise to Jesus Christ. I'm not sure what caused you to end up reading this book, but I'm delighted that you did. I like to think of our Father in heaven as being the One who somehow orchestrated all of this.

Now, however, our focus must shift from climbing to defending. More on this in a moment.

As we reflect upon our brief-but-important journey, there are some important things we must always remember. In a later chapter, I'll do a synopsis of the major concepts we've covered throughout this book so you can have an easy guide to refer back to. I'm hoping that if you've stayed with me this far, you may want to have an easy way to reference these simple concepts once in awhile—almost like doing some budgeting calisthenics. But for now, we need to absorb all of the savory benefits of what we've accomplished.

When I finally arrived at the summit of my own Mt. Budgeting, I was not only completely oblivious to the fact that I was actually on a budgeting quest in the first place, but it actually took a few decades to accomplish. Because it took so long, this has been more of a journey for me than a destination. For you, I hope just the opposite is true. As I write these very words, I wonder what my life would have looked like if I had learned and applied these lessons and concepts as a younger man. I really feel like my life would have looked a lot differently. It most certainly would have been financially more peaceful without all of those heartbreaking struggles with money—and with God. But if all of those struggles can now help any of you in any way, it will all have been worthwhile.

Arriving at the summit is not about learning new lessons. It's about fully absorbing all of the concepts we've covered during our arduous ascent. With that in mind, I'd like you to picture a huge wooden chalet at the summit of the mountain we've just climbed. Inside that chalet is a lovely sitting area with a crackling fire, which is framed by smooth, large river rocks forming a rustic fireplace. The vista out the nearby bay window is one where gray skies have now slightly parted and the sun is beginning to peek through the clouds. Surrounding the fireplace area are good friends, a nice cup of coffee, and some big puffy chairs. Your smart phone is turned off and you have absolutely nothing on your agenda for now. Oh, and Jesus Christ is also sitting in one of those puffy chairs, smiling and enjoying a cup of Joe with us during your graduation celebration.

Can you picture that? Good. Let's enjoy this moment together.

Base camp is a long way down the mountain and we don't ever want to go back down there. Actually, it's my sincere hope that you'll never descend that side of the mountain ever again. Although your ascent has been a series of sometimes difficult spiritual hurdles, you've now made it and nothing can make you go back down into non-budgeting bondage. Well, no one can put you back into bondage except <u>you</u>.

With that said, the first thing I'd like for us to reflect upon here at the summit is the subject of guilt. If any of you are feeling convicted by what you've been reading, please don't let Satan place a guilt trip on you about any of the previous mistakes you've made with money. It's merely a part of being human. Yes, having the conviction that you've not handled your money in an optimal fashion can drive you to want to change some bad habits. However, it should stop there. Don't forget what I've said. We're all born with our heart and money separated from each other, so you're not alone. Proper budgeting is a <u>learned</u> talent, not a natural one. In most cases, we must all ascend this spiritual mountain to find balance, peace, and joy with regard to how we view and treat our money. Rich or poor, we all need the contentment which can only come from being obedient to God with our finances. If you feel like you need to be forgiven for some older, bad monetary habits, ask Jesus for it. He's actually waiting for you. However, you must allow yourself to fully receive His forgiveness to successfully defend your position at the summit. Guilt can never come into the picture. Guilt is from the enemy.

No matter how much or how little money you make, once you've dethroned yourself as god of your wallet, the peace of the real God can now shine through. When you were trapped at the bottom of the mountain, you couldn't possibly see the sun through the thick cloud cover above. But now that you've made it to this lovely chalet, God's glorious light is penetrating the budgeting darkness.

But why is that? Don't you have to be wealthy to be effective with your money? How can you find peace if you don't have much money?

Once you've turned your financial focus onto Jesus Christ and therefore away from the world, your definition of financial success turns from the world's standard to God's standard. Can any of you right now tell me you wouldn't rather have God judge your heart when it comes to handling money than some random human's opinion? The world's standard is one where you must maintain a certain bank balance or you're considered to be a loser. Financial success in God's kingdom doesn't require a monetary entry fee, but the world's version of success certainly does. To me, it's unbelievably comfortable knowing I don't have to compare myself to others in some kind of twisted contest to see who can end up dying with the most money. Whoever dies that way actually ends up losing—big time.

On the other hand, God doesn't require your money or an entry fee. He only requires your heart. Truth be told, all of the money in the world belongs to the Lord, anyway. To me, it just doesn't make any sense to fight with God about money anymore. It's His money and if I want some more of it, I must first be a good steward with what I have. My desire for more money must also be for the right reasons. I must be an obedient son. I must also pray constantly for guidance. My motives must be noble and unselfish. I believe the same is true for you, also.

➤ Perspectives

As we bask in the lovely ambiance of The Summit's fireplace, I'd like you to consider giving yourself a grade in each of the chapters we've covered thus far. Undoubtedly, each of your scores will be unique and different. That's because God actually made each of us to be unique and different. Like I've said, in the last chapter of this book, I'll be highlighting some of the poignant moments of our journey together. You might think of it as a type of travel log.

For those of you who do go back and read each of the chapters again, I challenge you to grade yourself in each of them with honesty. Once you've accumulated your overall score, you'll then know the areas you need to work on. This will give you a roadmap to your spiritual strengths and weaknesses as it relates to money and budgeting. Perhaps this will help you with other spiritual situations, as well. Please remember that it's very difficult (or nearly impossible) to improve something you're not measuring. So go measure yourself to see how you're doing. Then, start improving on your weak areas. We all have them, for sure.

Another helpful way to visualize your financial journey is to envision the Mississippi River. When most of us hear the name of this magnificent waterway, we typically think of places like St. Louis, Memphis, and definitely New Orleans. These lovely cities have been founded on and have benefited greatly from the mighty Mississippi River over the years. But the Mississippi River doesn't start in Missouri, Tennessee, or Louisiana. No, it starts way up in Minnesota.

If you go to the headwaters of the Mississippi River, you'd probably not imagine it would turn into such a powerful waterway so far downstream. Its origins are humble, but its destination is magnificent. During its travel southward, many people are positively impacted by its presence. The Mississippi River is famous for many reasons, including its perseverance through difficult terrain and its ability to bless many people along its journey.

The same concept is true of your budgeting journey.

If you have humble beginnings right now, you have no idea how God may wish to use you once you've improved your budgeting trajectory. From the headwaters of my dual floppy disk computer to right now, a moment where I'm able to memorialize these experiences in a format where you're able to read them, my own Mississippi River has served my family well. Perhaps it's also helped a few others along the way. When I started my own financial journey, I had no idea you'd be reading about it in this book. Many times along the way, I felt sorry for myself. But now, I definitely know why God allowed it all to happen. You see, when you love Jesus Christ and experience tribulations, they can be turned into positive situations when the testimony of how God helped you ends up helping others.

As they say, that's my story, and I'm sticking to it.

My sincere hope is that your personal budgeting quest will continue to move from your own humble headwaters in the North Country to a magnificent delta on the Gulf of Mexico. Along your journey, Jesus will help you through your difficulties—if you allow Him to. Your own Mississippi River will be unique, to be sure. Remember, you're not alone during this journey. You may not be able to see your destination right now, but God certainly can. There is no way you can do this alone. God didn't design any of us to be a Lone Ranger. Don't be a macho knucklehead and try to go it alone. Life just doesn't work that way.

➢ My Story

Like most of us, every single day, I have a struggle between my human nature and my spiritual nature. Whenever I wake up and check all of our accounts over a cup (or two) of coffee, I always wish we had more money in savings. I always wish we had our house paid off. I always wish I didn't have to go to work that day because I've been working for a long time. But as this happens, the Holy Spirit, who lives in all saved Christians, always fires His retaliatory shots at these subtle fiery darts which constantly attack my human side. My humanity wants me to look at the world from its own, selfish perspective. This is a trap that must be avoided.

What I'm trying to tell you is that your version of "the accountant" will be under constant fire. Be prepared for this.

The responses to those "I always wish" items are usually the same. When I wish we had more savings, God fires back with, *you've been faithful with what you have, so I've got your back.* (Quick note … no, this isn't an actual audible experience. No, I'm not hearing voices. When God resides within you, and you actually listen to Him, you get feelings which move you towards God and away from the world).

Anyway, when I look at the balance of how much we owe on our house, I pray for God to help us pay it off instead of being scared we never will. And when I long for a day I can retire, I always feel immense gratitude for my incredible job with an outstanding employer who the Lord absolutely brought into my life. Essentially all of my daily "temptations" to worry are met with God's mighty hand. Although I can't stop these temptations from being fired at me from the realm of the demonic, I can shield myself from these attacks through my faith in Jesus Christ.

152

My point in all of this is that reaching the summit is difficult, but <u>defending</u> the summit is arguably more difficult (perhaps we'll tackle this issue in the next book). Just because you've made it here doesn't mean you can now put your financial life on cruise control. Instead, the battle has shifted. Although you're no longer climbing upwards with all of its spiritual struggles, defending your position now becomes the primary mission. While we've been struggling to climb this mountain together, we've been lugging our money with us to the top, which is where our heart for Jesus Christ is. Now that our heart and money have been united, our strategy of being on offense will now turn to defense.

So who are we defending our money against? Team Satan, of course.

I can assure you, the closer you move towards pleasing God, the more the enemy will come after you. Please remember that even the mighty archangel Michael wouldn't take on Satan without the power of God (see *Jude 1:9*). Just like Michael, you and I cannot take on the budget-hating enemy without the power of God helping to defend us. Trying to do so will undoubtedly result in pain and suffering. This isn't an issue of how strong each of us is. It's an issue of how spiritually humble we are. I suggest submitting to God daily in prayer and asking Him for protection for whatever you do. I pray constantly throughout every single day. I cannot win without Jesus helping me. Neither can you.

➤ RYB, Dude!

2 Timothy 4:7

KJV ... "I have fought a good fight. I have finished my course. I have kept the faith."

NIV ... "I have fought the good fight. I have finished the race. I have kept the faith."

➤ Actions

Let me ask you a question. What would happen to your body if your heart stopped beating this very moment? What would happen if your blood was no longer being pumped through your veins and arteries? The answer, of course, is that you would immediately keel over and die. That's how important your heart is. As we've discussed (perhaps ad nauseam), the same is true of your budget. If you develop a budget and don't continue to defend, watch over, and tend to it, it's like allowing your financial heart to stop beating. When your budgeting heart is no longer beating, your financial life will not perform optimally.

With that said, my action item for this chapter is simply this—N-S-B. That stands for "Never Stop Budgeting." Since you're at the summit, you can never stop budgeting or you'll likely fall back down to base camp.

> ## ➤ Let's Whiteboard That

"Relying on God has to start all
over everyday,
as if nothing has yet been done."
C. S. Lewis

15
Don't Look Down!

We're almost done, so this will be a fairly short chapter. It's just a quick caveat before we close out this book and send you towards budgeting success.

The basic concept I want to share with you now is that there's absolutely **no reason to go back** to where you've come from, so don't look down or you just might fall off of the summit. Once you've reached the summit, to return to base camp is far worse than to never have budgeted at all. To know the truth about the spiritual ramifications of budgeting and to fall back down to the world is unbelievably unproductive and will break your spirit. Don't do it. Please trust me—there's nothing left for you at the bottom of the mountain except a lot of frustration and heartbreak.

Many have shared with me that they have started a budget and have fallen away from it. This is probably due to the fact that many people have started a budget out of compulsion, not out of desire. When you feel forced to do something, the commitment to continue with it will inevitably fade. But when you really desire to commit to something, your heart has changed and the danger of falling back is minimal.

So at this point, I'd like you to consider committing your entire heart and soul to a budget. During our trek, I've tried to explain the "why" to you from my own testimony. If you start a budget as a New Year's resolution or to merely quell your guilt, it probably won't last. But if you run a budget as an act of worship of Jesus Christ, you won't want to stop budgeting, no matter what. And that's my entire purpose of writing this book in a nutshell.

In other words, I don't want you to commit to a budget. I want you to <u>want</u> to commit to a budget. This is obviously easier said than done. This is also why budgeting is actually a spiritual issue, not a physical one. In order to be successful in the long term, you must treat this spiritually, not mentally or certainly not emotionally. You can accumulate all of the <u>knowledge</u> of how to run your finances that you desire, but if you don't apply the <u>wisdom</u> of utilizing a robust and God-honoring budget, it'll be difficult to sustain the ongoing commitment it takes to be a committed, long-term budgeter.

➤ Perspectives

You can be rich and give back to God from your surplus, but that won't necessarily impress Him. On the other hand, you can be poor and give back to God faithfully, and you'll undoubtedly impress Him. In a similar way, if you're wealthy and don't think you need a budget, I'm afraid you're mistaken. If you're not wealthy and do submit to a budget, you'll ensure that your success if/when it comes later will be sustained forever.

It's a fallacy if you have money and think you don't need a budget. It's also a fallacy if you think by running a proper budget that you'll become rich one day. How much money you end up having in your life isn't the issue. You can't bribe God with your giving or impress him with your wealth. You can only honor Him with how humbly you view your money and whether you've committed to a budget which serves His kingdom. Gratitude is the key, here. To me, the hallmark of the Christian life is gratitude for what you have, not anger and frustration for what you don't have.

➢ My Story

Several years ago, my wife couldn't believe a string of words that came blurting out of my mouth one afternoon. To this day, she still cannot believe what I said to her that fateful day when we were browsing some stores at a nearby outlet center.

As we came upon a Clark's shoe outlet, I suddenly proclaimed, "Let's go buy some shoes." This was quite a shock to the both of us. To give you a little reminder, I act as our "accountant." That means I'm usually the one who squashes any splurges with reminders of where we are in our monthly expenditures.

But not that day. That particular day contained a brief, shining moment where it was time to cut loose a little. When I told Elissa we should go buy some shoes together, you could almost hear the old Steppenwolf tune, "Born to be Wild" playing in the background. To her credit, my wife just said "okay." I'm sure she was shocked beyond belief, but she just rolled with it. So with that proclamation, I revved-up my imaginary motorcycle and we entered the store. Undoubtedly, I was walking with a bit of a confident strut at that moment, and somehow thought I was being pretty cool. Each of us then proceeded to purchase a pair of shoes.

Yeah, I know. That's not a very impressive story on the manly-scale.

My point in sharing this is to remind you once again that budgeting doesn't mean you won't ever have fun and splurge once in awhile. To say you won't have fun with your money will almost undoubtedly ensure that you'll fall back down the mountain and quit budgeting. You need to have fun, for sure. It just needs to be done in a controlled manner. The truth is, when my wife and I splurge nowadays,

I feel so much better about it because it's occasional; not all the time. This makes it so much more enjoyable. By controlling our urges to constantly feed the furnace of our purchasing desires, splurges actually feel wonderful instead of guilty. Our God is a God of happiness, but we cannot achieve happiness without balance. We cannot achieve happiness without Him.

We all must remember to live by faith—I mean <u>true faith</u>, where you don't cling to your money like it's a life preserver. I can certainly understand the inclination to do so, but I also know it must be resisted and rechanneled.

➤ RYB, Dude!

Luke 21:1-4

KJV ... "And he looked up, and saw the rich men casting their gifts into the treasury. And he saw also a certain poor widow casting in thither two mites. And he said, Of a truth I say unto you, that this poor widow hath cast in more than they all: For all these have of their abundance cast in unto the offerings of God: but she of her penury hath cast in all the living that she had."

NIV ... "As Jesus looked up, he saw the rich putting their gifts into the temple treasury. He also saw a poor widow put in two very small copper coins. 'Truly I tell you,' he said, 'this poor widow has put in more than all the others. All these people gave their gifts out of their wealth; but she out of her poverty put in all she had to live on faith.'"

➤ Actions

Read the next chapter and get in the game. Don't forget the peace and comfort that comes from the union of your heart and your wallet as you remain at the lovely and peaceful chalet at the summit of Mt. Budgeting. Help others. Be happy with whatever God gives you. Love the One who gave you life. Be grateful for the One who also gave His life for you.

➤ Let's Whiteboard That

"You can have everything you want in life if you just help enough people get what they want in life."
Zig Ziglar

162

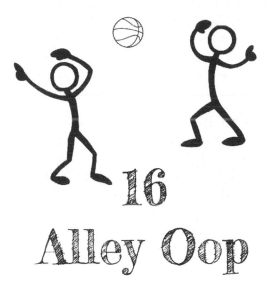

16

Alley Oop

In this, my closing chapter, I'll not be using the normal categories from the earlier chapters. We'll just "free form" it to close things out. This will essentially serve as a brief recap or travel log of our journey together.

To begin with, my desire and recommendation to all of you is that you take a comprehensive personal finances course—if you already haven't. The mission of those programs—in my opinion—is focused on the structure and techniques of building a personal finances platform. This is a very important skill set for someone to acquire. In my mind, to coin a basketball term, I'm pitching an "alley-oop" to one of the fine finance programs out there. They'll take you home. My job here is nearly done, so let's finish up.

From the beginning, I've said that my stated goal in this book is to work on your heart. Through my own story, I hope you were able to see some good reasons why you must focus on a budget so everything else in your financial life will work properly. Without question, **your budget is the center of your financial life—or at least, it should be** (maybe I should trademark that annoying saying).

All throughout these chapters, I've tried to make what I consider to be some very basic-but-critical points. These points have been emphasized over and over again. Of course, this was very much intentional. Although I never entered the military when I was younger (I almost did), I've always appreciated my friends who did. One common thing all of them shared with me was the interesting stories of going through basic training under the guidance of some hard-nosed drill instructors. Some of their stories were downright hilarious—at least, in retrospect, they were.

Anyway, it's always made sense to me that an effective drill instructor will constantly emphasize the basics in order for their recruits to absorb the essential techniques necessary to make them optimal soldiers or Marines, etc. This is an important survival technique for when the actual warfare begins. And yes, budgeting is absolute warfare against the world. That same concept holds true for the mission of climbing this mountain. To that end, I have intentionally emphasized what I consider to be the most important concepts several times throughout our journey together.

One quick note. Even though we're talking about basic training in the military, I'm not going to yell at you and insist you drop and give me fifty pushups. These days, I'm not sure I could do more than two, myself. I can't imagine asking you to do something I can't do.

Okay, so let's go ahead and close things out so you can get on to the business of effective budgeting. What follows are my closing quick hits:

Good budgeting isn't **rocket science** and it doesn't require any unique or special techniques. The spiritual aspect of budgeting is of paramount importance and must come first, before any of the normal budgeting or financial techniques will effectively work for the long term.

Happiness apart from God doesn't exist. Faithful budgeting brings **peace**, while ignoring it ultimately brings chaos. Comprehensive personal financial courses are an excellent way to learn **detailed techniques** on how to build your financial platform. I recommend investing in one.

Whether you make $10K or $10 million per year, faithful budgeting is for both **the rich and the poor**, as well as everyone in-between. It's understandable and even common to be broke, but it's not understandable to <u>not know</u> you're broke. It's also not okay to think you're too wealthy for budgeting. Good budgeting involves vision, which must first be stated and then followed. Don't allow money to be your god or your sanctuary of hope.

Jesus Christ wants our heart more than our wallet. He actually doesn't need our wallet. Jesus is not a **cosmic Santa Claus** who is merely here to shower you with whatever you want. He is God and He expects obedience. So keep an open mind and an open bible if you want to improve your budgeting skills. God will not compulsively force Himself on you. He asks you for your love and your commitment. The rest is up to you.

An effective budget is like the **plug** in your personal finances **bathtub**. With it, you can effectively use your money wisely. Without it, everything will possibly disappear by spiraling down the drain. Without a God-honoring budget, your money will certainly not last beyond your departure from earth—at least in a spiritual sense, it won't.

Do you want to change your bad budgeting habits? Since we're all born as a **wild stallion** with regards to our money, remember that faithful budgeting is a learned talent, not a natural one. Our wild side must be tamed and trained in order to be effective and to serve the Lord.

Bucket lists are awesome and most of us have one. But for the Christian, our **bucket list** lasts far beyond death's door. Living faithfully now actually ensures we have a fantastic bucket list for eternity. Life with Christ is never ending, so a Christian's bucket list never ends. Don't use your earthly desires as an excuse to over indulge yourself. God's kingdom is both vast and exciting. If you truly love the Lord, treat your money accordingly.

Your budget is to your personal finances like your **heart** is to your body. Every penny you have should flow through a God-honoring budget. Start the journey. Allow your budget to monitor every part of your finances like every drop of blood in your body repeatedly flows through your heart.

If you've hit **rock bottom** in your financial life, you're not alone. Do not fear, because <u>fear</u> belongs to the enemy. Persevere through hardship. Commit to budgeting because obedience is important to God. You can absolutely get out of the bottom of the financial well you've fallen into, but you must get off the couch and commit to a budget. This is an essential step.

Experiencing difficulties isn't necessarily punishment from God. If we allow Him to, our Father will **mold us** into the image of His son, Jesus Christ. We all must love God and love our neighbor. Being a son or daughter of God ensures that we're co-heirs of the entire universe and part of a royal priesthood. We must act like it.

Miracles happen every day, even in the seemingly smallest situations. Is there anything God can't do??? No. There's not.

Your budget is the **blueprint** of your financial life, but you must manage it with your heart for Christ. Blueprints don't make decisions—you do. God honors you by how much money goes into your budget. You honor God by what goes out of it.

When it comes to handling money, learn to be a **conduit**. A financial conduit transfers money from one place to another. Don't love your money, but do respect it. Remain balanced in all of your financial dealings. Life is not all about you and your desires. It's about God's eternal kingdom.

Marriages typically have a spender and a saver. Hire a mythical **accountant** to be the one who objectively shares with both of you just how much money you have. Keep the accountant <u>out</u> of the middle of your marriage, but let him/her be an objective part of it. This will help to unite spenders and savers.

Followers of Jesus Christ all have a **heavenly bank account** into which our spiritual deposits are made. This is important for eternal reasons. Are you living your life like a non-believer when it comes to your money—as if this world is all there is?

Your **earthly bank account** serves as your financial brain because it contains the intelligence (money) of your financial life. Respect it by balancing your checkbook. Save for future expenditures "old school" style by starting with small amounts and faithfully adding to it. When you're faithful like this, God usually gets involved and helps you if that is what He desires.

Be a **generous giver**, but don't give to simply receive. You're not on a quid-pro-quo basis with God. He is God and you are not. Don't give out of compulsion. Give generously because that's what sons/daughters of God do.

By all means, **have some fun** in your life, but be sure to maintain balance. Don't spend too much time having fun, and don't spend too little time having fun. Also, avoid the financial disease called binge shopping. Splurging once in awhile is wonderful. Splurging all the time ceases to be splurging at all. It's called self-indulgence and it's dangerous to your soul ... and your wallet.

Dreams and goals are important, but God must be involved. Perseverance is our response to God's gift of hope. Be a planner. Be a financial conservationist. Eliminate the negativity that accompanies the term "budget." Accrue money for your goals. Don't be a **Solomon** when it comes to chasing your dreams. He was at the top of the world but appeared to hate his life for it. Live your life honorably. The world has absolutely nothing to offer, but God does—through obedience to His commands.

Once you've reached **the summit** of your own personal budgeting quest, then relax and enjoy the peace that accompanies it. Don't allow the enemy to throw guilt at you for anything. Be faithful. Also, be prepared for spiritual assaults from the enemy. Jesus is there to protect you. Stay close to Him.

And lastly, don't just run a budget in order to manage your personal finances. Learn to **desire** to run a budget. Compulsory budgeting usually doesn't last. Joyful budgeting is obedient and pleases God because it focuses on Him, not on you.

I look forward to you perhaps reading these words again one day, but I sure don't want to see any of you down at base camp again. Once you've reached the summit, guard it with your faith. Defend it with your heart. Protect it with a strong, impermeable budget.

Your loyal tour guide (me) is now finished with his job. I'm heading back down the mountain to hopefully guide another group to the summit. I wish you all many blessings in the name of Jesus Christ....

Wade

PS ... I love dogs. I see God's creative genius and greatness in dogs. The only reason I'm mentioning this is because I talk about dogs in every one of my books. Mission accomplished.

Prayer of Salvation

I am excited that even seekers of biblical truth who are not yet committed to Christ would be drawn to this book, and I pray that your heart would be open to salvation. The amount of information now available for those seeking to find answers to their questions is nothing short of amazing. Finding faith in Christ is not about acting religious or having to dress a certain way. It's about surrender to the Creator of all that we see; the One who loves us more than we can imagine; the One who died for our sins; and the One who loves you, no matter what you have done.

It's important for you to know that it's absolutely normal to have questions and objections regarding matters pertaining to life in Christ. However, failing to truly seek the answers to your questions is extremely inadvisable. I ask you to consider going into an investigative mode, and to not let previous potentially false paradigms about matters of faith corrupt your journey. In other words, please go into your investigation with an open mind. I believe it will not be hard for you to find the answers to what you seek.

You must remember that only the Word of God is inspired by the Holy Spirit. Therefore, even though there are tremendous ministry tools available to aid you in your quest, they must always be synchronized with the Bible. If they fail to do so, they're absolutely false.

If you find yourself ready to find true joy for the first time in your life; if you're ready to change your days from hopelessness to hope; and if you're ready to secure your future for eternity; then please consider praying this simple prayer. If you pray this prayer in earnest sincerity, please understand that it's just the *beginning* of a long and incredibly enjoyable walk with the LORD. You'll need help along the way, so finding a local, Bible-based church with strong Christian leadership to disciple you in your walk is the next step.

Jesus,

I confess that I have sinned and fallen short of your glory.

I believe that you suffered and died on the cross for me,

And when you did that,

You paid the full price for the punishment due me, for my sins.

Please forgive me for my sins,

And accept me into your kingdom.

Until right now,

I have only lived for myself.

From now on,

I will only live for you.

Thank you for your incredible sacrifice,

And please also show me

How to help others.

When it is my time,

I look forward to being received

Into your glorious presence.

Please come into my life

Now,

And forever …

Welcome to the family!

Don't stop now, there's work to be done.

Biblical Verses Used or Referenced

Made in the USA
Columbia, SC
26 March 2019